ORIGINS AND DEVELOPMENT

of the

IRISH DRAUGHT HORSE

Colin A. Lewis

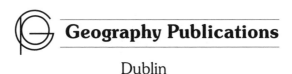

Geography Publications

Dublin

ISBN: 0 906602 475

Published in Ireland by
Geography Publications
24 Kennington Road
Templeogue
Dublin 6 W

Cover design and manuscript layout by
Bronwyn Tweedie

Printed by Leinster Leader
Naas
Co. Kildare

Title page illustration:
"The long car, 1984" from
Praeger, R. Ll., (1969) *The way that I went,*
The Collins Press, Cork

*As long as a man rides his hobby-horse peaceably and quietly
... pray, sir, what have either you or I to do with it?*

Laurence Stern (born in Clonmel in 1713),
The life and opinions of Tristram Shandy, Gentleman.

In memory of my friends of former years, my Irish hunters on which I enjoyed the unspeakable pleasure of galloping across the green grass in pursuit of the uneatable: Polly, Princess Stringy (8865), Dolly (whose registered Irish Draught name I have forgotten), and Champ, the bold Impeder gelding with the great big buck! And with gratitude to Billy and Fidelma Freeman for making it possible for me to engage in the horse life of Ireland.

FOREWORD

by
Dr Tom O'Dwyer
Chairperson, The Heritage Council

The Heritage Council is delighted to support *The origins and development of the Irish Draught Horse* under the Publications Grant Scheme of 2004. The Council has developed its own strategic plan for the years 2001-2005, a key element of which is the funding of high quality publications on aspects of Irish heritage.

At the core of the Council's ethos is the premise that individuals and local communities are the ultimate custodians of heritage. In order to obtain their involvement in the maintenance of their heritage it is essential to provide them with accurate and understandable information.

Professor Lewis has already published two highly praised books entitled *Hunting in Ireland* and *Horse breeding in Ireland and the role of the Royal Dublin Society's horse breeding schemes, 1886-1903*. He is congratulated on making information on the Irish Draught Horse readily and enjoyably available in his present book. The material drawn together in this publication will undoubtedly enrich the lives of those who are interested in the equine and equestrian heritage of Ireland.

Irish Draught Horses are a living part of our heritage and, as their value for sporting and recreational purposes is increasingly recognised, Council looks forward to expansion both in their popularity and in their numbers.

The Heritage Council,
Kilkenny,
Ireland
2004

ACKNOWLEDGEMENTS

Much of the research on which this book is based was undertaken in Ireland between 1970 and 1987. The author thanks the Librarians of the Royal Dublin Society and the staff of Bord na gCapall for their unfailing help during that period; the editor of *The Irish Field* for inviting him to write hunting features, the preparation of which necessitated riding and assessing the performance in the hunting field of many horses of Irish Draught and other breeding and introduced him to countless horse men and women throughout Ireland and elsewhere; the many owners who mounted him; the breeders and stallion men who freely imparted their knowledge; Mr N. O'Hare, then editor of the *Irish Draught Horse Yearbook*, for publishing the initial results of the author's research; and especially Joan C. Griffith, webmaster of the Irish Draught Horse Society, for including some of his publications on the Society's website, introducing him to recent research and thereby rekindling his interest in the history and development of the Irish Draught Horse.

Mr William Jervois of the Albany Museum in Grahamstown was an unfailing fount of information on Irish history, allowed the author free access to his library and was a constant source of encouragement and inspiration. Dr Charlotte Moore provided much pedigree information and her compilations: *Irish Draught stallions* and *Irish Draught mares*, are invaluable. Mrs Debi Brody of the Graphics Services Unit of Rhodes University, Grahamstown drew the maps and pedigree tables and scanned the illustrations. Miss Bronwyn Tweedie laid out the book. Mr Jervois, Professor Randall Hepburn and Mrs Marijke Cosser were kind enough to read and comment on earlier versions of the manuscript, although the errors that remain are the responsibility of the author alone.

Permission to reproduce illustrations was graciously granted by those listed in the captions. The author is particularly grateful to Mr N. O'Hare who, as editor of the relevant issues of the *Irish Draught Horse Yearbook*, encouraged him to include photographs previously published in that journal. Unfortunately it was not possible to trace the copyright holders of the poetry by W. H. Ogilvie or the map of Bianconi routes by T. W. Freeman: the author and publisher welcome any information that might enable them to do so.

The Heritage Council, Ireland, is thanked for a generous grant towards the direct costs of publication: without the support of that Council this book is unlikely to have been published. The Chairman of the Heritage Council, Dr Tom O'Dwyer, most generously wrote a Foreword to the book, for which the author is most grateful.

CONTENTS

LIST OF ILLUSTRATIONS

Figures

Tables

The hoofs of the horses! - Oh! witching and sweet
Is the music earth steals from the iron-shod feet;
No whisper of lover, no trilling of bird
Can stir me as hoofs of the horses have stirred.

On the wings of the morning they gather and fly,
In the hush of the night-time I hear them go by-
The horses of memory thundering through
With flashing white fetlocks all wet with the dew.

When you lay me to slumber no spot you can choose
But will ring to the rhythm of galloping shoes,
And under the daisies no grave be so deep
But the hoofs of the horses shall sound in my sleep.

Will H. Ogilve

Chapter One

INTRODUCTION

The development of stock breeding in Ireland, including that of horses, is inextricably interwoven with that of the social, economic and political life of the country. Technological developments, both at home and overseas, have also affected horse breeding, especially in the nineteenth and twentieth centuries.

The Irish Draught Horse developed as a light draught animal, suitable for carriage and other road work, for light farm work (including a limited amount of ploughing of soils that were not too heavy and sticky), and for producing the famous Irish Hunters when put to a Thoroughbred or good Half-bred sire. Many of the more athletic Irish Draughts were also competent hunters in their own right, to whom jumping seemed to come naturally. Above all, in the pre-motor era the progeny of Irish Draughts, and even Irish Draughts themselves, were ideally suited to military needs, and were greatly sought after by many of the armies of Europe as well as by the British army.

In the twentieth century the demand for army horses diminished, especially after the carnage of the First World War and the introduction of tank warfare. Tractors and motor vehicles also replaced draught horses on the land and on the roads and by the 1960s the future for Irish Draughts looked bleak. The growth of equestrian sports in the latter part of the twentieth century opened new avenues for the breed. Many horses bred from Irish Draught mares have proved themselves on the international show jumping scene and on the cross-country eventing courses of the world. At the same time Irish Draughts and some of their progeny are well suited to the needs of the riding school market. Thus, as mechanisation has replaced these impressive horses for farm, road and army work, so they have found new (though limited) outlets as sporting animals and the foundation stock from which non-Thoroughbred sporting horses are produced.

Ireland has been renowned for its horses for many hundreds of years. The present Irish Sport Horse thus comes from a long tradition of excellence. The development of that tradition is really the story of the Irish Draught, and it is a story that cannot be adequately told without reference to the economic, political and social conditions of the past. Additionally, Ireland has for many centuries had close links with the neighbouring island of Britain, and events in Britain have affected, and been affected by, events in Ireland. The evolution of the Thoroughbred, for example, is a story of the crossing of imported hot-blood

1

sires (such as Barbs, Spanish and Orientals) on native British, and Irish, Hobby mares. Similarly, the development of the Irish Draught appears to be linked to the introduction into Ireland of hot-blooded sires from England and elsewhere, as well as being a response to changing agricultural and transport needs in an evolving political and economic society.

The aim of this short book is to trace the development of the Irish Draught from the days of the famous Irish hobby horse to the present. In so doing reference is made to political, social and economic events in both Ireland and, to a lesser extent, in Britain. The careers of some of the leading people of the past are outlined, as are the great social and economic revolutions of the seventeenth and eighteenth centuries, such as the Cromwellian land settlements in areas such as County Tipperary, and the agrarian revolution of the eighteenth century and its effects upon agriculture, and hence horses, in Ireland.

Plate One: **Prince Henry (5)** (the number is the Irish Draught Horse registration number and is given hereafter after the names of all registered Irish Draughts listed in this book), foaled in 1890. This grey horse of 16.1 hands was sired by the unregistered **King Henry**. Photographed when 15 years old and the property of R. G. Cleary, Streamstown, Co. Westmeath. (Source: Irish Draught Horse Book)

The Irish have long been renowned as great horsemen, partly because of the skills that they have acquired in the hunting field, where some of the most daunting obstacles in the world are overcome with fluent ease on the part of both horse and rider. Attention is therefore paid to hunting and the Irish Draught horse, with particular reference to the work of the talented but little known early eighteenth century author, huntsman and naturalist: Arthur Stringer.

Little, if anything, is known of the pedigrees of Irish Draught type horses before the very last years of the nineteenth century, but paintings and other works of art provide ample evidence that Irish Draughts have existed in Ireland for many years. The work of many artists is thus referred to in this book, and examples of their depictions of Irish horses, some of which were obviously of Irish Draught type, are included.

Since 1730 government support, and later that of the Royal Dublin Society, has been given to non-Thoroughbred horse breeding in Ireland. The horse breeding schemes of the Society, and of the government, are thus briefly discussed. From the *Register of Stallions* and other documents it has proved possible to map the distribution of Irish Draught horses at various stages during the twentieth century. It has also been possible to map imported stallions in the mid-eighteenth century and, just as important, to plot the distribution of non-Thoroughbred horses in Ireland in the latter years of the twentieth century and to graph the ages of the brood mare herd. Genetic studies of Irish Draughts at the turn of the new millennium have shed much light on the composition of this now endangered breed, and are described.

The formation and role of the Irish Draught Horse Society, which is perhaps the most influential body concerned with the future of the breed, is also described and the breed standard and guideline stated. Finally, the pedigrees of the major foundation-stock sire lines are given, as are illustrations of many of the Irish Draughts of the past and of the people who, in some way or another, have played roles in the development of Ireland's own breed of warm-blooded horses.

The Irish Draught, an endangered breed: long may it survive and delight the hearts of horsefolk throughout the world!

Chapter Two

PONIES, WAR HORSES AND THE IRISH HOBBY

Introduction

Ponies were widespread in Ireland in early Christian times, as evidenced by carvings on High Crosses, such as that at Ahenny on the borders of Tipperary and Kilkenny (Lewis, 1980a). Larger, cob-like horses were apparently introduced to the country by the Anglo-Norman invaders in the twelfth century and records of horse breeding in the next two centuries exist from areas of pronounced Anglo-Norman influence, such as County Wexford (Lewis,1980a).

Plate Two: *Horsemen and chariot, from the eighth century High Cross at Ahenny in Co. Tipperary.* (Photo: courtesy of the Commissioners of Public Works in Ireland)

Hobby horses and exports

During the fifteenth century Ireland was starting to be renowned for the production of horses. In 1517 the Bishop of Armagh reported to King Henry VIII that Ireland "...produces absolutely nothing but oats and most excellent, victorious horses, more swift than the

English horses"(Mackay-Smith, 1983). In 1577 Richard Stanihurst noted three types of horses in the country: the Hobbie "of pace [amble] easie, in running wonderful swift"; horses for military service: "...they amble not, but gallop and run"; and the third sort: "...a bastard or mongrel hobbie - strong in travelling, easie in ambling and verie swift in running"(quoted from Mackay-Smith,1983; an ambler is a horse that moves both legs on one side simultaneously, giving a level ride, unlike the bumpy ride produced by a horse that trots).

In the sixteenth century the 9th Earl of Kildare and the 9th Earl of Ormonde and Ossory (the latter of whom died in 1581) "...both kept large studs for the breeding of Hobbies which they raced also in England" (Lewis, 1980a). Henry VIII imported Irish Hobbies for his own racing stables in England in 1531 while Lord Kildare presented him with more Hobbies in 1532 (Mackay-Smith,1983).In January of that year the 8th Earl of Ormonde and Ossory wrote that he was sending a Hobby to Henry's Chief Minister of State, Thomas Cromwell (Mackay-Smith,1983).

Plate Three: *Tomb of Piers Rua Butler (died 1539), 8th Earl of Ormonde and Ossory, and of his wife, Margaret Fitzgerald, in St Canice's Cathedral, Kilkenny. In 1532 the Earl wrote that he was sending a Hobby to Thomas Cromwell, Henry VIII's Chief Minister of State.* (Photo: courtesy of Bord Fáilte)

Irish Hobbies were also sought after by Italian and other European noblemen. In 1498, for example, King Henry VII wrote to the Duke of Ferrara to tell him that Irish horses were on their way to him but that "...from the present turmoil and constant wars of the wild Irish amongst themselves, there is, forsooth, a great scarcity there of good horses" (Lewis, 1980a).

Political unrest in the Sixteenth Century

During December 1532 the Earl of Kildare was wounded in battle in Ireland. Subsequently he was summoned to London, charged with using the King's artillery for the defence of his own property, and imprisoned. His son, Thomas, promptly rebelled against the King, only to be executed in London, with five of his uncles, in 1537. The Earl had already died, in 1534. The 1530s were also years of momentous change in the relationship between state and church. In 1533 Henry VIII repudiated Papal jurisdiction and supremacy over his kingdom. In the following year, by an Act of the English parliament, Henry became "Supreme Head of the Church of England" (MacCurtain, 1972). These events and their aftermath resulted in much unrest in Ireland, culminating in a policy of destroying the power of many of the existing and mainly Catholic landowners and replacing them with Protestant English settlers: the so-called Plantations.

The remainder of the sixteenth century was marked by unsettled conditions, which are unlikely to have been conducive to the development of horse breeding except in favoured areas. In 1579, for example, the 15th Earl of Desmond, whose lands were essentially in south western Ireland, within the Province of Munster, rose against the Crown.

Plate Four: *An Irish chieftain, possibly the 15th Earl of Desmond (circa 1538-1583), with his ambling Hobby held by a groom. Notice that the horse is shod only on the hind feet, probably to encourage it to put most weight on its hindquarters and thereby sprint faster than if it had been shod all round. American Quarter Horses, which race over very short distances (originally quarter of a mile) and may be descended from Irish Hobbies imported into Virginia in 1666, are also normally only shod behind.* (From John Derricke's *Image of Ireland,* published in London in 1581)

He was assassinated in 1583. His lands were confiscated and his stud at Rathkeale, in County Limerick, passed into English hands, although the breeding of Hobbies is known to have continued there until at least 1666. In that year the then owner, Sir Thomas Southwell, exported one stallion and four mares across the Atlantic to the colony of Virginia (Mackay-Smith,1983).

In 1581 John Derricke depicted an Irish chieftain with his horse, held by an attendant, in the background. The horse is shown in the ambling position and may well have been a Hobby, since Hobbies (as Stanihurst had noted) were amblers. The chieftain's horse appears to be of about 15 hands, deep in the girth, with powerful and rounded quarters, well sloped shoulders and muscled forearm, somewhat short and over-arched neck, smallish ears and rather common head. This is a horse that was obviously up to considerable weight and that would have been well able for farm work.

The Munster Plantation and the importation of livestock

There is little doubt that, during at least the latter part of the sixteenth century, horses and other farm stock were imported into Ireland from England. Under the Munster Plantation, that began around 1586, large parts of that Province were divided into seignories of 12,000; 8,000; 6,000 and 4,000 acres which were allocated to English 'undertakers'. Sir Walter Raleigh, for example, obtained lands in County Waterford and

Plate Five: *Youghal in the later sixteenth century. This was one of the ports through which horses were imported into Ireland, probably in vessels like that on the right of the illustration.* (Redrawn by A. R. Orme from the original published in *Pacata Hibernia* in 1633, reproduced courtesy of Professor Orme and the Geographical Society of Ireland)

later added another 40,000 acres in Cork, Tipperary and Waterford. Raleigh's possessions included the port and market town of Youghal. In 1604 he sold these lands to Sir Richard Boyle, the First Earl of Cork. Boyle "... founded the frontier towns of Bandon, Clonakilty, Enniskean and Castletown to hold the settled country against the Irish of West Carberry (Co. Cork) and Kerry" (Freeman, 1950). Another settler, who met with less success than Raleigh and Boyle, was Edmund Spenser, the poet. He obtained an estate of some 3, 000 acres at Kilcolman, near Doneraile, but retreated to Cork and then to London after 'the Irish' burnt his dwelling! These, and other settlers, must have introduced English ideas of agriculture, and English livestock, to Ireland. Thenceforth, if not before, the history of horse breeding was not that of Ireland alone but of England and Ireland.

Chapter Three

THE SEVENTEENTH CENTURY:
HOBBIES AND THE DEVELOPMENT OF WARM-BLOODS

Introduction

The seventeenth century was one of the most disturbed periods in Irish history, with the beginning of the Ulster plantation (1608-10); the rising of 1641; the execution in London in 1649 of King Charles I and the subsequent campaigns and land confiscations in

Plate Six: *Oliver Cromwell (1599-1658), leader of the Parliamentarians, who led his troops in a bloody campaign in Ireland in 1649-50. Engraving from a painting by Robert Walker.* (Source: Lodge, 1827)

Ireland of Oliver Cromwell (1649-50); the restoration of Charles II in 1660 and the resultant partial restoration of land in Ireland to its former owners; and the Jacobite war (1688-1691).This war ended in the Treaty of Limerick of October 1691, with the transportation of some 14,000 Irish soldiers from their homeland to France. Under King William, who had defeated the Jacobites, there were further confiscations of land (1691-1703). In 1695 came the infamous Penal Laws that discriminated against Roman Catholics.

Success in horse breeding, as in many other forms of economic activity, depends to a large extent upon peaceful conditions and other suitable circumstances. In 1610 an appeal was made to the Corporation of London to provide settlers for the 'Derry plantation, claiming that the countryside there was suitable for all kinds of husbandry and for the breeding of horses and cattle (Freeman,1950). Much of Ireland was suitable for horse breeding, given peace and stability.

Cromwell, the restoration of the Monarchy and stability

There are various ways in which stability may be assessed. One is by examining the installation, pillage and destruction of church bells. Bells are expensive and require considerable skill in design and manufacture. They are unlikely to have been produced in areas that were disturbed and war-like.

Between 1600 and 1659 only 17 bells are known to have been installed in Ireland, none of which were located west of a line from 'Derry to Cork (Dukes,1994). In 1649-50, under the Parliamentarians, Oliver Cromwell and his troops destroyed or pillaged some of the wealth of eastern Ireland. St Peter's Church in Drogheda, where the defenders of that town had fled after Cromwell's men broke through the town wall, was blown up and the tower burnt: "...men and bells [came] down together, the most hideous sight and terrible cry". The bells of Selskar Abbey in Wexford were looted after that town was captured. In Kilkenny the Cathedral was damaged and Cromwell took away "...five great and goodly bells". Who could think of horse breeding at such a disturbed period?

After the Restoration of the Monarchy in 1660 conditions became very different. Bell ringing was popular among leading intellectuals and society men in Restoration England, especially in London, Norwich and the Oxford area (Cook, 1987) and attempts were made to develop it in Ireland. In 1668 a ring of six bells was hung in the cathedral in Waterford. In the 1670s at least 42 bells were installed in Ireland, including three rings in Dublin, one in Limerick and one in Kilkenny. Only 18 bells were apparently installed in the 1680s, including the ring of six bells at Blessington. By the 1690s, after the troubles caused by the Jacobite wars, the number of bells installed fell to nine, although they included one ring, at Clonmel.

The period of peace and prosperity in Ireland in the seventeenth century, as suggested by the installation of church bells, was essentially limited to the latter part of the century and especially to the 1670s. The earlier part of the century, judged by the evidence of the bells, cannot have been too prosperous and conditions were probably ill suited for major agricultural developments, including much progress in horse breeding.

The Irish Hobby

In 1609 Nicholas Morgan wrote that "The Irish Hobby [is] a Horse of middle size, comely and well shaped, and of much courage and fury" (Mackay-Smith,1983). A more useful description, albeit relating to English Hobbies, was given by Michael Baret in 1618: "...of good stature, somewhat large but not very high, a small head, full eye, wide nostril, a pricke ear but somewhat long, a firm thin crest, with a long straight necke, well compact on the cragge at the setting-on of the head, a broad breast, deep chested, a round backe, being barrell ribbed and the short ribs shot up somewhat close to the hucklebone [point of the hip], the buttocks somewhat long, so as to be proportionable, a flat legge and straight foote, and hollow hoofe" (Mackay-Smith, 1983).

By the 1630s Hobbies were in short supply in Ireland. Entries in The Calendar of State Papers attributed this to so many having been exported, but this is probably only part of the story. When Laurence Esmonde wrote from Dublin to Lord Dorchester in 1630 he merely stated facts and carefully avoided offering explanations: "There is nothing worthy presenting your Lordship, for the dainty breed of Hobbies, which were here, are quite gone" (Mackay-Smith,1983).

The English Hobby

Francis Barlow (1626-1704) produced a number of drawings of English Hobbies, both at pasture and racing. These animals were probably similar to Irish Hobbies, which had been imported into England for racing and breeding purposes for many years. Barlow's drawing of a race near Windsor Castle in August 1687 shows rather cobby animals of about 15 hands, heavily muscled, with convex heads and short necks, that were not markedly dissimilar from the coach horses standing in the background of his composition. This picture was subsequently engraved and is considered to be the first English racing print (Mitchell, 1985). As Mackay-Smith (1983) commented, the race horses have "...no appearance of Oriental blood," unlike eighteenth century paintings of racing scenes at Newmarket, the Curragh and elsewhere. Six years later, when Theodore Maas sketched the Battle of the Boyne (1 July 1690) he drew horses that were obviously hot-blooded and Thoroughbred in appearance.

Barlow's India ink drawing of English Hobbies at grass, which was published as an etching in 1663, is particularly important for students of the Irish Draught. The Hobbies have fine and proud heads set on crested and well-arched powerful necks with long, flowing

Plate Seven: An English Hobby. Etching by Wenceslas Hollar (1607-1677) after a drawing by Francis Barlow (1626-1702) published in a book entitled *Variae Quadrupedum Species* in 1663.

manes, well sloped shoulders, moderately deep girthed and rounded chests with plenty of room for heart and lungs, rounded and muscular hindquarters with rather low-set tails, short substantial and rounded cannon bones, well sloped pasterns on the hind but somewhat short and upright on the fore, and only a little feather on the legs above the pasterns. The hoofs are well sloped, and look trim and hard. Although scale is hard to judge, the trees in the background indicate that the Hobbies were of about 15.2 hands, or perhaps a little more. They look very much like Irish Draught horses of the early twentieth century, if, perhaps, a little lighter and smaller.

The Irish horse

The Irish horse of the 1660s has been described as small but "...full of mettle, exceedingly hardy, and will carry burdens the greatness whereof would startle any man's belief" (MacLysaght, 1939). Among other uses they "...continued steadily to displace oxen for draught use"(MacLysaght,1939), although horses had been used for tillage, at least for harrowing, since 1285, or even before, in County Wexford (Lewis, 1980a).

The Irish garron

In the seventeenth century, and more recently, garrons (small horses) in Ireland were hitched by their tails to a swing plough in teams of six or eight. The advantage of tail-hitching, though barbarous and declared illegal, was that the team stopped rapidly when the plough hit an obstacle, such as a stone or a root. This reduced damage to the plough (and probably to the horses' tails!). Each horse normally had its own leader "...and it is not hard to imagine the shouting and swearing and the constant stops and restarts which marked the slow progress of the plough as it turned its uneven furrows" (MacLysaght, 1939).

Plate Eight: A Dublin 'car horse' of the late seventeenth century, harnessed to a 'Ringsend coach.' Ringsend was then a village on the coast of Dublin Bay, beside the mouth of the River Liffey. The horse has the ambling gait typical of Hobbies. (From Dingley, Observations in a voyage through the Kingdom of Ireland)

The height of typical garrons is suggested by the minimum height required in the 1660s for car horses (horses pulling passenger vehicles for hire) in Dublin:15 hands. Nevertheless it is said that "...they were generally passed if over fourteen hands" (MacLysaght, 1939).

Hunters and carriage horses

Of course, there was more than one type of horse in Ireland in the seventeenth, as in previous centuries. In 1670 Colonel Daniel O'Brien sent to Lord Arlington, a Secretary of State to King Charles II and a most influential politician, "...a gelding that I have some time tried after the hounds, and although he be of an Irish breed, I think he will not be left behind by any company that hunts in England". This Irish Hunter is most unlikely to have resembled the typical garron!

O'Brien, who wrote from County Clare, claimed that "I begin to be the greatest breeder of horses in the King's dominions for I keep about my house 16,000 acres for my mares, colts, and deer" (MacLysaght, 1939). That there was a market for quality horses suitable for hunting and carriage work is indicated by the fact that, in the same year in which O'Brien put pen to paper, "...the Countess of Ossory [was] escorted into the City of Dublin

Plate Nine: *Staplestown, Co. Carlow, where Sir William Temple had his estate, as drawn in the 1670s. (From Dingley, Observations in a voyage through the Kingdom of Ireland)*

by sixty coaches, most of them with six horses" (MacLysaght, 1939). The Countess was daughter-in-law of James, 1st Duke of Ormonde (Burke,1939), who did much to improve the quality of horses in Ireland.

Sir William Temple and the improvement of horse breeding

Although Colonel O'Brien and others obviously bred horses of quality, by 1673 Sir William Temple considered that the standard of Irish horses needed attention. Sir William, who possessed an estate at Staplestown in County Carlow, had represented Carlow in the Restoration Parliament in Dublin in the 1660s. He had then been appointed an envoy plenipotentiary of King Charles II on the continent between 1665 and 1679 (Watson,1969). During that period he pondered ways in which Irish trade could be expanded.

On 2 July 1673 Temple addressed to the Lord Lieutenant of Ireland an Essay upon the Advancement of Irish Trade. Sir William wrote that "Horses in Ireland are a Drug, but might be improved to a Commodity, not only of greater use at home, but also fit for Exportation to other Countries. The soil is of a sweet and plentiful Grass which will raise a large Breed; and the Hills, especially near the Sea coasts are hard and rough, and so fit to give them Shape and Breath and sound Feet"

Temple was concerned particularly with the development of race horses in Ireland. He envisaged that racing horses over long distances and carrying large weights, would encourage breeders to improve their animals, thus making Irish horses more useful, and internationally marketable, than hitherto.

In 1665 King Charles II had instituted races in England known as the King's Plates. They took place over four miles, "Every horse that winneth three heats shall win the plate or prize - every rider carrying twelve stone weight...besides bridle and saddle - and every horse shall have half an hour's time to rub between each heat" (Mackay-Smith, 1983). The number of winning heats was later reduced to two for most King's Plates.

Temple proposed that the King should give two Plates to be raced for annually and that the Lord Lieutenant of Ireland should: "For Honour", be present at those races. Furthermore, the owners of the winning horses should "...be admitted to ride from the Field to the Castle [i.e. Dublin Castle, the seat of governance at that time in Ireland] with the Lord Lieutenant...and to Dine with him that Day....This to be done what quality soever the Persons are of; for, the lower it is, the more will be the Honour...and the encouragement of breeding will by that means extend to all sorts of Men". In due course King Charles II gave two Plates, which were raced for annually, in April and September, at the Curragh (Watson,1969).

Match racing, where one horse raced against another, was popular especially on the Curragh in pre-Temple days. In April 1634, for example, "Lord Digby and the Earl of Ormond [sic] matched each other's horses there over four miles, and the great Earl of Cork in backing Lord Digby lost 'a new beaver hat to Mr Ferrers, one of the Lord Deputy's gentlemen" (Welcome, 1982).By the end of the century racing was so much in vogue that "On the Curragh there were...several fine horses kept hereabouts for the race in stables built on purpose" (Cullen, 1968). For success in the new long-distance heavy-weight heat contests, such as those envisaged by Temple, perhaps more so than in the old-style match contests, it was important that horses should have at least some hot (Oriental, Barbary or Spanish) blood.

Plate Ten: *King Charles II (1630-1685), who established four-mile long flat races known as King's Plates that did much to improve the quality of race horses in England and, later, in Ireland. Engraving from a painting by Sir Peter Levy.* (Source: Lodge, 1829)

The importation of hot-blooded horses and the initiation of the Thoroughbred

Hot-blooded horses were imported into Ireland in the seventeenth century, as witnessed by a letter of 1668 from the Duke of Ormonde to his stud manager at Carrick-on-Suir. Ormonde mentioned both an Arab and a Spanish stallion at that stud (Lewis, 1980a).Unlike Hobbies, which ambled, hot-blooded horses trotted, as do modern Irish Draughts. Nineteen years later, in 1687, Lord Ossery paid £129 for a well-bred horse at a time when the annual average income for a lawyer was £154 and that of farmers and shopkeepers "...about £45" (MacLysaght, 1939). Such an expensive animal could hardly have been a garron! Lord Ossory was only sixteen years old when he bought those horses. He was a grandson of James, 1st Duke of Ormonde (Burke,1939).

Although no detailed contemporary description of Irish race horses of the match era apparently exists, in 1598 von Loehneisen wrote about English racers of that time. In translation, he stated that:

"In England there are good durable horses...held in great regard in German courts - especially for racing. Those which serve this purpose have the following characteristics: they are thin of body, fairly tall and, in addition, long in the shank, broad flanks, high thighs, narrow chest and therefore move more lightly and are more handy for racing". von Loehneisen added that: "The best racing horses in England come from the stud of Sir John Fennings [Fenwick] and are trained there" (Mackay-Smith,1983).

Plate Eleven: *Sir John Fenwick (1579-1658) of Wallington, Northumberland, breeder of 'The best racing horses in England' in the seventeenth century and Surveyor of the Race (stud manager) to King Charles I at the Royal Stud at Tutbury in Staffordshire. Sir John was knighted in 1605 by King James I, was Member of Parliament for Cockermouth and for the County of Northumberland and sat during the Long Parliament but was excluded for being too supportive of King Charles I. He was created a Baronet by that King in 1628.* (Courtesy of the National Trust for Places of Historic Interest and Natural Beauty, owner of Wallington, in which this portrait hangs)

von Loehneisen's description of English race horses of the period around 1600 shows that at least some of them already resembled Thoroughbreds: thin of body, long in the shank, broad flanks, and so on. They bore little resemblance to the racers depicted near Windsor by Barlow in 1684. Sir John, however, came from Northumberland, in the north of England, and during the seventeenth and early eighteenth centuries that area, and particularly the Vale of Bedale and the Helmsley region of north Yorkshire, was the nucleus within which Thoroughbreds were developed.

The Earls of Rutland, whose stud was at Helmsley, used Hobby mares "as a foundation for producing bigger and speedier race horses" (Fairfax-Blakeborough, 1950). These mares were bred to sires of a type known as Turks that had been imported from the eastern Mediterranean since at least the sixteenth century. Sir John (1579-1658) not only had his own stud of race horses, but was also Surveyor of the Race (stud manager) at Tutbury, in Staffordshire, which was the principal stud farm of King Charles I. The Royal Studs were closed and the horses sold after the execution of the King in 1649 (Mortimer *et al.,*1978). The horses that Barlow depicted racing near Windsor in 1684, which was far distant from the Yorkshire area where Thoroughbreds were being developed, may thus have been of the older, Hobby, racing stock.

The letter of 1668 from the Duke of Ormonde to his stud manager proves that, within ten years of the death of Sir John Fenwick, if not before, Oriental stallions were being stood at stud in Ireland. In fact, in 1650 Ormonde is believed to have "...bought six of the best horses from the dissolution sale of the Tutbury Royal Stud...brought the horses to Kilkenny and put them...to the local mares" (O'Hare, 1978). The breeding of horses is thus unlikely to have lagged appreciably in Ireland behind that of England. Sir William Temple may thus have been overly pessimistic when he described horses in Ireland as "...a Drug"! Judging from Colonel O'Brien's letter of 1670, and the number of coaches that accompanied Lady Ossory's entry into Dublin that year, in the seventeenth century Ireland must have produced a considerable number of warm-blooded horses of quality in addition to the race horses that were Temple's immediate interest.

The Duke of Ormonde and Anglo-Irish connections

The close links that existed in the seventeenth century between some of the leading families in Ireland, and between Ireland and England, are epitomised by the life of James Butler, the 12th Earl and first Duke of Ormonde (Airy,1886). Some of his linkages, as already indicated, proved beneficial to the furtherance of horse breeding in Ireland.

Plate Twelve: *James Butler (1610-1688), the 12th Earl and 1st Duke of Ormonde, sometime Lieutenant-General of the Horse, Commander- in-Chief of the Forces and Lord Lieutenant of Ireland. Ormonde was a major breeder of horses who bought stallions from King Charles I's stud 'and put them... to the local mares' in the Kilkenny area. In 1668 he had an Arab and a Spanish stallion at his stud at Carrick-on-Suir. Ormonde was also Chancellor of the Universities of Dublin and of Oxford and did much to encourage the economic development of Ireland. Engraving from a painting by Kneller.* (Source: Lodge, 1829)

In spite of his Irish connections Butler was born at Clerkenwell, in London, in 1610. His infancy was spent at Hatfield, in Hertfordshire, just north of the capital city. In 1613 he travelled to Ireland where he lived until 1619. James then returned to England, where he fell in love with and married his cousin, the only daughter and heir of the Earl of Desmond.

From 1630-32 James lived at Carrick-on-Suir with his grandfather, Earl Walter. During this period he commanded a troop of horse and so became familiar with the equine requirements of the army. On the Earl's death in 1632 James inherited the title and promptly travelled to Scotland and England. From 1633-47 Ormonde was mainly in Ireland, but moved to England in the latter part of 1647. In 1640 he had been made Lieutenant-General of the horse and Commander-in-Chief of all the forces loyal to the Crown in Ireland. As such, in 1641and subsequent years he took up arms against those who rebelled against the Crown in Ireland.

Plate Thirteen: *The Butler castle and Elizabethan manor house at Carrick- on-Suir, home of James Butler's grandfather, Earl Walter. The manor house was built by 'Black Tom', the 10th Earl of Ormonde, who '...was kept at the English court until he was 22' (Craig,1982). Tom hoped to entertain Queen Elizabeth I at Carrick-on-Suir. The gallery-hall on the first floor of the manor house contains stucco work with the initials TO and ER, presumably intended to signify at least the friendship between the Earl and his monarch. The style of the manor house is similar to that of many buildings in the Cotswolds of England and it is obvious that 'Black Tom' was familiar with English domestic architecture and introduced it to Ireland with this fine house. James Butler, the 12th Earl of Ormonde, was equally familiar with England and English ways of life, and with developments in horse breeding in that sister isle, as his introduction of stallions from England indicates.* (Photo: courtesy of Bord Fáilte)

Ormonde was in close touch with King Charles I and his son, King Charles II, and became a Privy Councillor following the restoration of the monarchy. During the Parliamentary period he had dealings with Oliver Cromwell. In 1648 Ormonde travelled in England and France before returning to Ireland in September. In 1650 he was in France, 1655 in Germany, 1656 in what is now Belgium, 1657 Germany, and so on. Ormonde was thoroughly used to travelling and to mixing with many of the leaders of society in various countries.

Ormonde must have been thoroughly conversant with developments in horse breeding in England and probably in other countries as well, at least insofar as they related to military and transportation needs. He was also in a position to influence developments himself. In March 1661 he was created Duke of Ormonde in the Irish peerage, adding that honour to such titles as the Earl of Brecknock that he held in the English peerage. During the 1660s Ormonde was on the Commission for the Treasury, Chancellor of both Oxford and Dublin Universities, Lord High Steward of England, and had extensive estates and agricultural interests in Ireland. These included at least one stud farm. By using hot-blooded sires on at least the more suitable of the local Irish mares, the Duke fostered the production of warm-blooded horses of military and other value.

Definition of a warm-blood horse

Dent (1978) has defined a warm-blood as a horse that has its origin "...in a cross of hot-blooded Oriental or Mediterranean stock on the cold-blooded North European...horse". The quality hunters and carriage horses of seventeenth century Ireland presumably contained Barb, Turk or other Oriental genes and were warm blooded. Dent (1978) has argued of warm-blooded breeds that "The Cleveland Bay is the only such breed in the British Isles, where its closest affinity...is with the Irish Draught Horse". The Irish Draught is warm blooded and native to Ireland, and probably developed in the seventeenth century as Oriental and Mediterranean sires were imported and serviced indigenous Irish Hobbies, both racing and, as Stanihurst so inelegantly put it, "...bastard or mongrel [but] strong in travelling". In so doing the native ambling Hobbies were presumably converted into trotting carriage, military, light draught and general purpose farm horses: in fact, into Irish Draughts.

The Penal Laws

Towards the end of the seventeenth century, in 1695, the Penal Laws attempted to control the ownership of horses of quality and to penalise the religious majority in Ireland: "No Papist, after the 20th of January, 1695, shall be capable to have or keep in his possession, or in the possession of any other, to his use, or at his disposition, any horse, gelding or mare, of the value of £5 or more" (Lewis, 1980a). This law should have had severe repercussions upon horse breeding, since the vast majority of the people of Ireland were adherents of the Roman Church, but there is little evidence that it did so. Instead, especially in fertile areas like much of County Tipperary, in which English settlers had been established in previous years, agricultural and social life flourished.

Cromwellian settlers and the rise of the country gentry

Nolan (1985) has shown that a group of Cromwellian soldiers and adventurers settled in County Tipperary in the second half of the seventeenth century. Some of them, like other entrepreneurs in that County, prospered sufficiently to build country seats during the following century. Over 180 "gentry seats" were shown in Tipperary on the maps of Skinner and Taylor of 1778. These were essentially agricultural estates with a "Big House" and many of their owners must have been dependent upon agriculture for their well being. Under those circumstances, horses suitable for agricultural as well as carriage, light draught and other work, must have been essential.

Plate Fourteen: *Sopwell Hall, Cloughjordan, seat of the Sadleir family. The house was probably designed by Francis Bindon (circa 1690-1765).* (Photo: courtesy of The Irish Georgian Society)

Sadleir of Sopwell Hall, near Cloughjordan, probably typified many of the Cromwellian settlers. Colonel Thomas Sadleir named his house after his father's residence in Hertfordshire, just north of London, thus emphasising the links between the fertile lands of Tipperary and those of England. By 1745 the Sadleirs had amassed enough wealth to erect an impressive two storey house, probably designed by Francis Bindon (Bence-Jones,1978). Bindon was an intimate of Jonathan Swift, the renowned writer, political campaigner and Dean of St Patrick's Cathedral in Dublin; Thomas Sheridan the actor and impresario who was a leading figure in the theatre in London and Dublin; and Dean Delaney whose wife, Mary, was a well known letter writer, painter, gardener and designer (Garner,1983; Crookshank and Glin,1987). The Sadleirs were thus in touch with cultural developments elsewhere in Ireland and in England, and presumably they were equally in touch with developments in agriculture, including horse breeding.

Chapter Four

THE EIGHTEENTH CENTURY:
A CENTURY OF PROGRESS

Prosperity and the importation of horses

Prosperity during the eighteenth century not only enabled Irish owners to build impressive houses, like that of the Sadleir's at Sopwell Hall (and many others that were

Plate Fifteen: *The Godolphin Arabian, by George Stubbs (1724-1806), engraved by his son, George Townley Stubbs. Stubbs was one of the most renowned of all horse and sporting painters, as well as being an anatomist, but he may have exaggerated the tremendous crest of the horse. Since Stubbs painted this picture in the 1790s and The Godolphin Arabian had died in 1753, Parker (1971) suggests that he probably relied on existing portraits,(such as those by James Seymour, John Wootton, David Morier and James Roberts), rather than on his own fading memories, although it is uncertain whether Stubbs had ever seen the horse!*

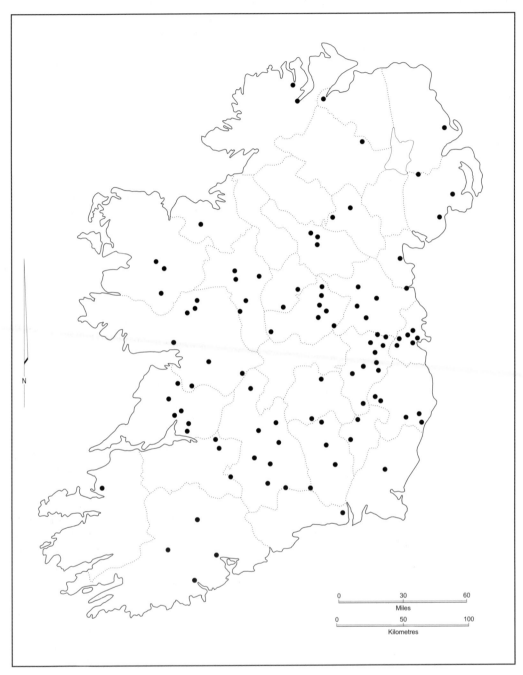

Figure One: *The location of imported stallions standing at stud in Ireland in 1750. Each dot represents one stallion. Stallions also stood at the following places but have not been mapped because it was not possible to identify the locations positively: Ballinamona, Ballyfad, Ballymaddock, Belrath, Crossdoney, Frankford, Heath, Ireland's Grove, Killinaul (Fermanagh), Pateswell. (Redrawn from Lewis and McCarthy,1977; courtesy of The Geographical Society of Ireland)*

much finer) but also to import increasing numbers of horses. In 1742, for example, six mares from Morocco were landed at Cork, while by 1750 over one hundred imported stallions stood at stud in Ireland (Lewis and McCarthy, 1977). Among the imports were horses of the highest quality, such as the "...fine bay six-year-old stone horse, got by Lord Godolphin's Arabian" that was brought into Ireland in 1752 (Cox, 1897). Lord Godolphin's Arabian is one of the three ancestors to which all Thoroughbreds trace in the male line, the others being the Darley Arabian and the Byerley Turk, which Colonel Byerley rode at the Battle of the Boyne in 1689 (Moore,1981).

The agrarian revolution

Prosperity was due, at least in part, to two major economic revolutions that took place initially in England: that of agriculture and that of industry. Of these, the agrarian revolution, led by such men as Jethro Tull (Clare,1899), came first. Tull (1674-1741) was born in Berkshire but commenced farming on his own behalf near Wallingford, in Oxfordshire. In about 1701 he invented a seed drill. After moving to another farm, in Berkshire, Tull travelled in France and Italy, observing agricultural methods in both areas. He was impressed by the success of hoeing between the vines that he saw in Languedoc and determined to introduce similar hoeing on his own farm. In 1731 he published a specimen of his work entitled *Horse-hoeing Husbandry*. This was immediately pirated in Dublin and seems to have met with a ready readership: at least the more anglicised farmers in Ireland had little intention of being left behind their counterparts in England in agricultural developments.

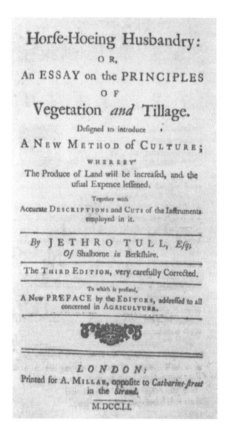

Plate Sixteen: *Title page of Jethro Tull's Horse-Hoeing Husbandry, first published in full in London in 1733. Tull invented a drill for sowing seeds in rows, which gradually replaced sowing broadcast. An advantage of sowing in rows was that weeds between the rows could be hoed with a horse-drawn hoe, the prongs of which moved between the sown rows.*

Even if Tull's work had not been pirated and made available to readers in Ireland it is likely that his methods would have been introduced rapidly by people like Sadleir, whose family connections in England were with the adjoining County to that in which Tull farmed. Tull's farming techniques entailed the use of horses for light tillage work. That meant that light, rather than heavy draught horses, were needed for Tull-type drill and hoe cultivation, although heavier horses, or even oxen, were useful for ploughing. The sale of Tull's publication in Dublin strongly suggests that light draught horses were available, or were soon bred, to undertake his sort of cultivation on at least some of the more progressive farms in the country.

This four Wheel Drill Plow, with a Seed and a Manure Hopper, was first Invented in the Year 174. and is now in Use with Wm Ellis at Little Gaddesden near Kempstead in Hertfordshire, where any person may View the same. It is so light that a Man may Draw it, but Generally drawn by a pony or little Horse

Plate Seventeen: *Horse-drawn seed drill of the 1740s.*

The Dublin Society and premiums for horses

In 1731, the year in which Tull's pirated work was sold in Dublin and the year after the Irish Parliament passed an Act for the Encouragement of Tillage, the Dublin Society was founded. This Society was intended to aid the development of agriculture and industry in Ireland and to be a scientific society (Lewis, 1980a). In 1820 it became the Royal Dublin Society. The birth of the Society took place during a period of rapid economic advancement, exemplified by the building of major country houses. These included the seat of William Conolly, great uncle of Tom Conolly the huntsman and race horse owner, at Castletown in County Kildare, the erection of which began in 1719; Westport House in County Mayo, built around 1730; and the extensive alteration of Carton House in County Kildare between 1739 and 1745. These developments were made possible by economic progress under peaceful conditions, following the unrest of the previous century.

As the years progressed the Dublin Society fostered progress via the incentive of premiums. Premiums were financial grants intended to aid development. The initiation of premiums for horses in Ireland appears to have been the work of individuals, other societies, and government. In 1747 the Provost of Trinity College Dublin, 'Premium' Madden, offered a premium of £20 for the importation of suitable mares. In the following year Government Commissioners appointed under an Act of 1730 offered premiums for the importation of Black Horses. These were the foundation stock from which breeders, particularly in England, were to produce heavy draught Shire Horses (Chivers, 1976). In the same year the Limerick and Clare Society gave premiums for the best draught filly and the best draught colt exhibited at its Show. Heavy draught horses, it was believed, could replace oxen for ploughing in clay and other heavy soils, and for heavy draught. They were not likely to replace light draught horses for carriage, light tillage and similar work.

In 1768 the Dublin Society awarded premiums to Thomas Johnson of Tipperary for the importation of "...six strong able mares fit for the plough and other country work, and

Plate Eighteen: *Castletown, Co. Kildare,begun in 1719. This was the seat of William Conolly, Great Uncle of Tom Conolly the huntsman and race-horse owner.* (Photo: courtesy of Bord Fáilte)

from four to six years old." The Society gave gold medals that year to the Earl of Shannon, who had imported both mares and "...a fine black stallion." The Earl farmed in the fertile region near Castle Martyr in County Cork, just as Johnson farmed a fertile area in County Tipperary. Robert French, whose family still owned over 12, 000 acres in County Roscommon in the 1880s (Bateman,1883), was the recipient of a premium for the importation of another "fine black draft stallion" (Fell,1991). It is thus apparent that appreciable efforts were being made in the eighteenth century to upgrade the standard of draught horses in the productive light arable lands of Ireland that stretched northwards from just east of the city of Cork, through Tipperary and into the limestone lands of the midlands of the country. Whether the Society intended the imported horses to upgrade existing stock to heavy draught status, or to increase the quality of existing light draught horses, is unclear.

In 1800 premiums were awarded under the patronage of the Dublin Society for the importation of horses "...of the Suffolk Punch breed." Lord Lucan, who owned tens of thousands of acres in County Mayo and a handful in County Dublin, was said to be "...the pioneer of Suffolk Punch importation" (Fell,1991). Significantly, perhaps, the Suffolk Punch is a smaller and more compact draught horse than the Shire or the Clydesdale, is essentially clean-legged and is generally considered a more active animal than its compatriots of the other two breeds. In the latter years of the eighteenth century the Suffolk Punch was developed into a coach horse, although many of the heavier draught type remained.

Plate Nineteen: *Notice the largely clean-legged appearance of this Suffolk Punch stallion, which is very different from the feathery legs of Shires and Clydesdales.* **Colony Millennium (8891)**, *owned by Mr and Mrs J. Fleming of Eyke, was foaled in 2000, by* **Colony Edward (8781)** *out of* **Colony Elite (28322)** *and was photographed at Woodbridge Show in 2004. Although Suffolk Punches are presently associated with agricultural use, in the eighteenth and nineteenth centuries a lighter type of Suffolk was developed as a carriage horse. Premiums were awarded in 1800 for the importation of Suffolk Punches into Ireland.* (Photo: courtesy of the Suffolk Horse Society)

In 1784 The Reverend Sir John Cullum described Suffolk Punches as "... *about fifteen hands high, of a remarkably short and compact make; their legs bony and their shoulders loaded with flesh. Their colour is often of a light sorrel... They are not made to indulge the rapid impatience of this posting generation; but for draught they are perhaps unrivalled... With wonder and gratitude have I seen them ... drawing my carriage up the rocky precipitous roads of Denbigh and Caernarvonshire*". Arthur Young wrote in 1797 that "... by aiming at coach horses the breed is much changed to a handsome, lighter and more active horse".

Suffolk Punch horses have been renowned for centuries for their equable temperaments and their chesnut/light sorrel colour. All present-day Suffolk Punches trace back to Crisp's Horse of Ufford, foaled in 1768 and advertised as a stallion "...able to get good stock for coach or road" (Ewart,1960). This stallion stood 15.2 hands high, had "...low fore end, large carcase, short legs and bent hocks, and perhaps a less inelegant head than most of his contemporaries" (Biddell, 1880).

Plate Twenty: *Arthur Young (1741-1820), who is generally considered 'the greatest of English writers on agriculture', worked in Ireland from 1777-9. In 1780 he published his Tour in Ireland, providing important descriptions of Irish agriculture. In 1784 Young founded a monthly publication named Annals of Agriculture, for which wrote most of the leading agriculturalists of the day (including King George III, 'Farmer George').* (Courtesy of The Albany Museum)

Agriculture in the second half of the eighteenth century

Arthur Young (1741-1820), the English agriculturalist and writer, worked in Ireland from 1777-9 and toured much of the country (Higgs, 1900). He described how, in County Cavan, Lord Farnham "...sowed his turnips and cabbages with a drill and horse-hoed the weeds... although oxen were used for ploughing and general draft work." Farnham was a landowner who had previously farmed in Norfolk, which was one of the main centres of agricultural innovation in England. Presumably Farnham used light draught horses for drilling and hoeing, although Young confusingly added that "Lord Farnham also bred work-horses." Perhaps that meant that he bred heavy draught horses, although his use of oxen suggests that they were lighter draught animals.

The importance of tillage, even in a County such as Tipperary, which was grazier rather than ploughman-land, is shown by the farming enterprises of Catholic Irish middlemen who rented their lands from landlords (Nolan, 1985). John McCarthy, for example, held his land from the Earl of Clanwilliam. McCarthy farmed in the Golden Vale, where Arthur Young visited him during Young's sojourn in Ireland (1777-9).

According to Young, McCarthy occupied some 9,000 acres, had over 11,000 livestock, 200 acres of tillage and employed between 150 and 200 workers. On such a holding there must have been ample work for horses of Irish Draught type, which would have been valuable for light tillage work (such as a limited amount of ploughing, and for harrowing, drilling, hoeing, and so on), for light cartage and as riding animals suitable for stock and other work. The fact that Irish Draughts could jump, gallop and follow hounds, must have been an added advantage in an area where there were many hunting packs.

Riding to hounds in the eighteenth century

Wyndham-Quin (1919) has written that, in County Limerick around 1750: "...almost all of the larger gentry owned a pack of some kind, with which they would hunt either stag, fox, or hare". Around the foot of the Galtee Mountains, which rise above the Golden Vale in which McCarthy farmed, in 1750 or thereabouts "...within a space of 34 miles...not less than 20 packs of buckhounds were to be found, each pack being kept by the owner of a deerpark." To hunt such a country, then as now, called for horses of bone and substance, able to cope with the heavy going of the soft and water-logged winter lands and with scope and sense enough to negotiate the streams and ever increasing banks and ditches of an increasingly utilized countryside. An Irish Draught type horse, or better still, the progeny of a hot-blooded sire on an Irish Draught type mare, would have been well suited to follow hounds in such countryside.

Hunting had been common in Ireland for many centuries, but as the native woodlands were cleared, especially during and after the seventeenth century (McCracken, 1971), so it increasingly adopted its modern sporting character. As the already quoted letter of 1670 by Colonel O'Brien indicates, huntsmen had no intention of being left behind, they wanted horses that could jump, stay and gallop, no matter what the going or the obstacles. Brian Merriman, the racy poet from County Clare, expressed the feelings of huntsmen in his poem in Irish dating from about 1750, which has been translated as *The Midnight Court;*

> *This view would bring the heart to life-*
> *Be it worn with sickness, age, or strife*
> *The sound of the horn and a glimpse of the hunt*
> *With the pack in chase and the fox in front.*

Lewis (1975) has shown that: "By 1750 private packs of kennelled hounds followed on horseback had been formed in Counties Armagh, Clare, Cork, Down, Galway, Limerick, Kildare, Meath, Tipperary, Waterford, Westmeath, Wicklow and probably in Dublin." The Duhallow, a subscription pack in County Cork, is generally recognised as the first pack to regularly hunt foxes in Ireland, which the pack was doing by 1745. To negotiate the wet winter lands of Duhallow required, then as now, horses able to cope with deep going and major obstacles, such as half or three quarter breds out of Irish Draught type mares.

Arthur Stringer's ideal hunters

Arthur Stringer was huntsman to Lord Conway on His Lordship's estates between Lough Neagh and the River Lagan in County Antrim during the initial decades of the eighteenth century (Fairley, 1977). The Conways had been granted their Irish lands in 1610, by King James I, under the Plantation of Ulster. To those lands they probably introduced settlers from their English estates, in Warwickshire.

In 1714 Stringer published *The experienced huntsman*, which Fairley (1977) considers "...the earliest treatise on hunting in Ireland". This book appeared nineteen

THE

Experienc'd *Huntfman*,

O R,

A COLLECTION of

OBSERVATIONS

Upon the Nature and Chace

Of the {
Stagg,
Buck,
Hare,
Fox,
Martern and
Otter.

With fome particular Directions con-
cerning the Breeding and Entring
of Hounds :

Alfo the Qualifications and Conduct of an
Huntfman, and Inftructions to a *Park-
keeper.*

All gathered from the Experience of Thirty Years
Practice.

_____

By Arthur Stringer.

_____

Belfaft, Printed by *James Blow,* 1714.

Plate Twenty-one: *The title page of Arthur Stringer's book, which was first published in Belfast in 1714. James Blow, the printer, moved from Glasgow to Belfast in 1694 where he established the first printing business in that town. The book was republished, with minor alterations, in Dublin in 1780. In 1977 it was again republished, in Belfast, edited and with an introduction by James Fairley of the Department of Zoology of University College Galway. Fairley considered Stringer's book to be 'the first treatise on hunting in Ireland, the earliest reliable book on the Irish Fauna and, most importantly, the first serious work to be devoted to the wild mammals of these*

years before *An essay on Hunting* was published in England and sixty seven years before Peter Beckford's classic *Thoughts on Hunting* was published in that country. Paget (1899), obviously with hunting in what was then the United Kingdom in mind, incorrectly wrote that "There had been no text-book on hunting previous to [*Thoughts on Hunting*]" having overlooked *An essay* and Stringer's work.

Stringer wrote that "He who resolves to hunt foxes must ...keep very good horses, and in good plight...in as good keeping and order as a horse for a race." Stringer dedicated the initial part of his book to The Earl of Mount-Alexander, writing: "That we have hounds and horses...in this part of the kingdom is in good measure owing to your lordship's great example in breeding most excellent in both kinds." That Stringer knew the importance of good horses for hunting is shown by various of his statements, such as "...to...keep near your hounds, you ought to be well mounted." Like many huntsmen, Stringer suffered from thrusters who, in trying "...who hath the best horse...ride upon the very heels of the hounds."

Unfortunately Stringer did not describe the sort of horses used for hunting in his area, but his book clearly indicates that care was taken in breeding animals that had to be capable of "...leaping a ditch, swimming a river, or venturing over or through a bog." Stringer's ideal hunter also had to be sensible enough to be led over "...an extraordinary leap" and to allow his rider to dismount "...where a horse cannot ride", so that the huntsman may proceed on foot "...through mountains, bogs and rank coverts." Additionally, a good hunter had to be able to stay: "...for a fox will run sometimes ten, fifteen or twenty miles...I have...run foxes twelve, fifteen, or sixteen miles from where I unkennelled them." Stringer also mentioned the need for "..a strong horse and car" in order to convey the body of a stag that had been caught and killed.

Stringer's ideal hunter: able to leap, swim, stay, get through bogs and deep ground yet be sensible and quiet enough to lead when necessary, sounds far more like a warm-blood than a hot-blooded Thoroughbred. The final part of Stringer's book consists of a dialogue between two imaginary gentlemen, who discuss hunting. One complains that the sport is overly expensive and that "...gentlemen have sunk their fortunes and ruined their families by it." The other, sensibly, replies that "Hunting is not an expensive diversion if men would keep themselves within just bounds of it. I keep twelve couple of good hounds and have four good nags which I particularly appropriate for that purpose, and find the expense very moderate." Assuming that the gentleman hunted hounds himself, and had to mount himself and one servant, his horses were probably expected to hunt at least once a week, if not twice. Stringer must, therefore, have assumed that hunters would be sound and capable of hard work. In other words, Stringer's ideal hunters were probably warm-blooded Irish Draughts, half-or possibly three-quarter breds.

Artists and the depiction of horses

Although no pedigrees of warm-bloods appear to have survived in Ireland from the eighteenth century, by the 1740s artists were depicting hunting scenes in various parts of the country and these indicate that warm-bloods were reasonably widespread, at least on the hunting field (Crookshank and Glin,1978). Heavy looking hounds and short-coupled, muscular, deep-girthed horses that were well up to weight, appear in at least some of the paintings. These include the work by an unknown hand entitled *George first Lord Carberry and his Hounds*, in which hounds persue an antlered stag across a river, with a horseman in full flight jumping a stone wall. Joseph Tudor's *View of Blessingtown* (Blessington), which was probably also produced in the 1740s, shows similarly close coupled but smaller horses,

Plate Twenty-two: 'A north prospect of Blessingtown, County Wicklow'. Engraved in 1745 by John Brooks from a painting by Joseph Tudor (?1695-1759). Notice the conformation of the horses, which is similar to that of many present-day hunters in Co. Wicklow. The mansion in the middle distance was built of brick towards the end of the seventeenth century by Michael Boyle, Archbishop of Dublin, to whom the manor of Blessingtown had been given in 1669 by King Charles II. The mansion was burnt down circa 1760. (Photo: courtesy of the Public Record Office of Northern Ireland)

such as would have been suited to the hilly country around that town. These were obviously warm-bloods and not remarkably different from some of the hunters that might be seen at present with the Shillelagh or other local Hunts, being either small Irish Draughts or their half-bred progeny.

By 1768 Robert Healy was drawing long necked and obviously hot-blooded, if rather small and fine boned hunters in his depiction of Tom Conolly's *Castletown Hunt*. The leg markings of a couple of the horses suggest that they were at least partly of Arab blood, while the huntsman standing beside one of them shows that at least some of the hunters were little over 15 hands high. Conolly's pack hunted in County Kildare and adjacent parts of Dublin and Wicklow. Healy's picture, like the magnificent oil painting *The Death of the Hare* that is now attributed to him but was formerly thought to be by Stubbs, shows little evidence of Irish Draught or half-bred type blood in the hunting horses. Significantly, with the exception of a curbed lady's mount in *The Death of the Hare*, the horses are depicted wearing snaffle bridles, which is traditionally a more common form of harness for Thoroughbred and other hot-blooded stock than the double bridles that used to be popular for warm-blooded hunters.

Plate Twenty-three: *'Tom Conolly and his hounds' by Robert Healy, 1768. Conolly lived at Castletown, Co. Kildare, the building of which had been commenced in 1722 by his Great Uncle, William Conolly. William, who became Speaker of the Irish House of Commons, was considered the richest man in Ireland in his day. Notice that the horses depicted with Tom Conolly's hounds are obviously hot-blooded. The leg markings of two of the horses on the right are typical of those of Arabs. Judging by the man standing by his mount, and the length of stirrups of those already mounted, the horses were little more than 15 hands high.* (Courtesy of The Hon. Desmond Guinness and photographed by J. Harsch. The original painting is now in the ownership of the Yale Center for British Art, Paul Mellon Collection)

Although the pedigrees of carriage and other light draught horses used in Ireland in the eighteenth and earlier centuries do not appear to exist, pictures of them survive from at least as far back as the 1730s. In the next decade a coach and six is seen approaching Stradbally Hall in County Leix (Crookshank and Glin, 1978).

Unfortunately the individual horses are so small on the painting that little can be discerned about their conformation. By the 1780s far more instructive paintings were being produced, such as William Ashford's *Carriage passing Frascati*, which is near Blackrock in County Dublin. The horses are well built and active (and one of the leaders is rearing) and the picture was painted in 1781. In the early years of the following decade

Plate Twenty-four: *Six horses, that appear to be light draughts, trot with a carriage along an Irish road, circa 1737.* (From *The Journal of George Edward Pakenham, 1737-9*)

Plate Twenty-five: *This depiction by James Malton (died 1803), of Powerscourt House in Dublin, shows riding and carriage horses that are not unlike Irish Draughts, although their tails have been docked.*

James Malton produced a series of views of Dublin, which give clear impressions of what street scenes were like. Double bridled and rather heavy and well built riding horses that appear to be 15.2 hands or less in height, are depicted in the vicinity of Powerscourt House in Dublin. In front of the house stands an elegant carriage with a team of four well groomed horses. All the horses in this scene are obviously warm-bloods and are not unlike twentieth century Irish Draughts.

Francis Wheatley, in his 1781 masterpiece: *The Dublin Volunteers on College Green*, mounted his horsemen on strong but small Irish Draught like animals. In spite of their restricted height (they cannot have been much over 15.2 hands, if as tall), the horses are up to considerable weight and appear full of mettle, with their alert faces and rounded haunches. Fifteen years later similar, but perhaps somewhat heavier and larger horses, were depicted by Thomas Robinson at a procession in Belfast. These and other works show that Irish Draughts were well developed as a type, even if not as a breed, by the latter part of the eighteenth and the early part of the nineteenth centuries. Joseph Peacock's *Festival of St Kevin at the Seven Churches, Glendalough,* exhibited in London in 1817, shows countrymen on typical Irish Draughts gossiping at the fair, while vehicles drawn by what appear to be Irish Draughts try to force their way through the multitude.

The increase in road transport

Carriage and other road transport was made increasingly possible in Ireland during the eighteenth century by the widespread improvement of many of the roads. Andrews (1964) has written that "Before the latter part of the seventeenth century, Irish roads seem to have been neglected for several centuries." In 1710 the first Grand Jury road act was passed and from then on new roads rapidly increased in number. Under the Grand Jury system new roads could be built as long as the Grand Jury of the relevant County was convinced that they were necessary and agreed to raise the money needed for their construction.

Grand Jury roads

The problem with Grand Jury roads was that there was little incentive for any Jury to agree to roads linking Counties since they were paid for by a cess (tax) on the individual County through which the portion of the road ran. Consequently long distance routes tended to be neglected. To counteract this problem, in 1729 the Irish parliament adopted the English system of turnpike trusts. This system provided new roads throughout much of the country and led to considerable improvement in the condition of some existing roads, thereby facilitating road transport and providing an incentive for the breeding of light draught horses suited to coaching and other work.

Turnpike roads

By the beginning of the nineteenth century turnpike roads radiated from Dublin to Cork, Limerick, Coleraine and the main towns in the midlands, such as Roscommon, Birr and Nenagh. In 1790 the first Irish mail coaches were introduced, and some of the roads were improved to cater for the fast moving mails. The result was that, for much of the eighteenth century, there was a ready market for horses suited to road transport and, especially, for light draught horses such as those of Irish Draught type. This was in great contrast to the previous century, when many roads were in such bad condition that "...hardly any public coaches were in existence and wheeled traffic was in constant difficulties....Pack horses were much used, and in the remoter parts of the country these

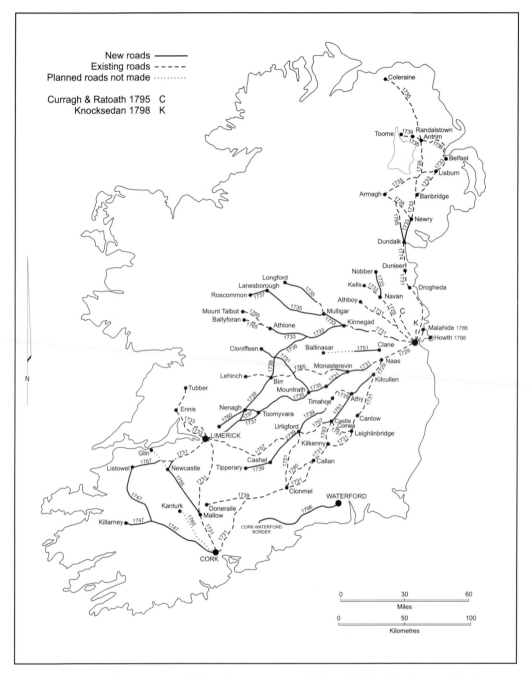

Figure Two: *Turnpike roads established by Acts passed before 1805. The dates of the Acts are shown.* (Redrawn from Andrews, 1964, courtesy of The Geographical Society of Ireland)

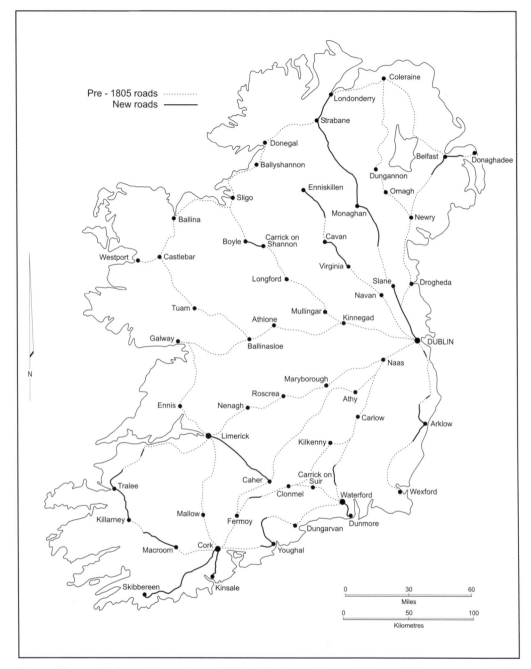

Figure Three: *Mail coach roads in 1832.* (Redrawn from Andrews, 1964, courtesy of The Geographical Society of Ireland)

represented the normal and indeed almost the only form of transport" (MacLysaght, 1939).

Road vehicles and the need for light draught, coach and carriage horses

According to Cullen (1968), in the 1770s "...500 cars have been seen in a line transporting wool from Ballinasloe to Cork." Each 'car' was pulled by one horse, was two-wheeled and probably carried up to 12 cwts (600 kg). In the same decade there were, in and around Limerick, 183 four wheeled and 115 two wheeled carriages. Early in the following century Samuel Frederick Brocas painted *A view of the Courthouse and St Mary's Cathedral, Limerick* that included a four wheeled carriage drawn by two sturdy trotting horses. They could well have been Irish Draughts, even if not so-called at that time. In the late 1700s "In Fermoy, on the main road between Dublin and Cork, horses were provided for six mail-coaches every day", in other words, at least 24 coach horses were stabled at Fermoy for the mails, alone. The market for light draught horses of carriage and mail coach type was therefore extensive in the eighteenth century.

Plate Twenty-six: *A one-horse cart typical of those in Ireland in the late eighteenth century and that might have transported 'wool from Ballinasloe to Cork'.* (Drawing from the notebooks of Joshua Gilpin, 1796)

Canal horses

Another source of employment for horses was the canals, which, from 1756 onwards, began to extend across Ireland from Dublin to the River Shannon. Other navigable waterways, such as parts of the system of the River Barrow, had already existed for many centuries. The barges on the canals were towed mainly by horses, at least until steam power was introduced. Passenger boats, called Passage-Boats, which were succeeded by lighter Fly Boats, were towed by "swift" horses. Some cargo barges were hauled by a single horse. McIlroy (2003) has described how "A well-trained horse always knew to put his shoulders forward into the collar before taking a step to start towing the barge."

By the 1830s Fly Boats travelled at eight miles per hour and the contractors who supplied horses for their haulage are known to have purchased hundreds of animals for this trade (Delaney,1973). The passenger boat horses, judging from various illustrations (Delaney and Delaney,1966), were light draughts. They worked four to a boat, harnessed in pairs with the near side draught being ridden by a horse boy.

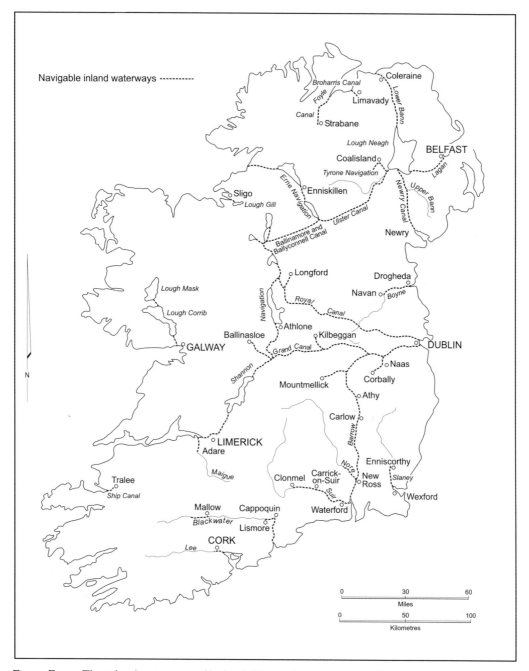

Figure Four: *The inland waterways of Ireland. Waters that were navigable in the nineteenth century are shown by dashed lines.* (Based on Delaney and Delaney,1966)

The end of the century

In the last decade of the eighteenth century came the horrors of the French Revolution, to be followed by the Napoleonic Wars. The British army needed horses for the cavalry, mounted infantry, artillery and commissariat and there was a booming trade for over a decade. Breeders even produced horses suitable for various army needs, so much so that in 1836, over twenty years after the war ended, it was held that "...the standard of horses had progressively deteriorated ever since they were no longer bred for military use" (Bianconi and Watson, 1962).

Plate Twenty-seven: *A passage (passenger) boat on the Royal Canal, pulled by four light draught horses, leaves Dublin in the 1840s. The barge on the right appears to carry a cargo of turf (peat), which was in great demand as a source of fuel in the city. (Engraving from Hall and Hall, 1841-3)*

Chapter Five

THE NINETEENTH CENTURY:
ROAD TRANSPORT, POLITICS AND HORSE BREEDING

Bianconi's passenger services and the use of Irish Draughts

In 1815, following the end of the Napoleonic War, an Italian entrepreneur, Charles Bianconi, began a passenger service from Clonmel to Cahir with "...a sturdy animal bred for hauling artillery limbers" (Bianconi and Watson, 1962). In the years that followed Bianconi extended his services throughout much of Ireland, and by 1836 his vehicles were travelling 3,800 miles per day and were worked by more than 1,300 horses, which he bought in Ireland. These were all light draught horses, working at speeds of eight to ten miles per hour including stops. All harness used by Bianconi "...was of standard dimensions; for Bian's [i.e. Bianconi's] horses were, as far as possible, of the size known in the army as "troopers", standing at 15 hands 2 inches". In other words, Bianconi apparently used Irish Draught type horses.

Fortunately Bianconi arranged for Ackermann, the London firm of art dealers, to publish a set of six aquatints from drawings by Michael Angelo Hayes (1820-77), entitled *Car Travelling in the South of Ireland in the year 1836 - Bianconi's Establishment.* These show teams of both three and four horses pulling four-wheeled side cars, which were commonly called 'Bians'. The depiction of *The arrival at Waterford* shows two greys, a wheeler and the lead horse, and a bay or liver chesnut. The leader is drawn in the pacing position, even though the team is pulling up and the wheelers are on their haunches. There is no sign of feather on the legs of any of the team, which are well muscled with strong but sloping hindquarters. The leader may well be mistaken for an Irish Draught of the latter part of the twentieth century, like *Legaun Prince*, who stood in County Tipperary in the 1970s and 1980s.

Youatt's description of Irish horses

In 1843 William Youatt published a description of Irish horses: "The Irish horse seldom has the elegance of the English horse; he is larger headed, more leggy, ragged-hipped, angular, yet with great power in the quarters, much depth beneath the knee, stout and hardy, full of fire and courage, and an excellent leaper. It is not, however,

Plate Twenty-eight: Charles Bianconi (1786-1875), the Co. Tipperary entrepreneur, born in Italy, who used many thousands of Irish Draught type horses to pull his passenger vehicles. (Courtesy of Mrs S. J. Watson)

Plate Twenty-nine: One of Bianconi's passenger vehicles. Notice how the horses resemble many modern Irish Draughts. (Engraving from an aquatint of 1836 by Michael Angelo Hayes; 1820-77)

the leaping of the English horse,...it is the proper jump of the deer, beautiful to look at, difficult to sit and, both in height and extent, unequalled by the English horse." These were the sort of horses that worked the Mail Coaches and the Bians, the carriages of the gentry and the traps and floats of many lesser mortals. Some of them were also ridden to hounds, at least occasionally, while a large number worked on ordinary Irish farms. They had not yet been honoured by the title Irish Draught Horse, neither had their pedigrees been committed to any stud book, but that was probably because the era of the stud books, apart from *The General Stud Book,* which was for racing stock, had not yet arrived either in Ireland or Britain.

The recording of pedigrees

The recording of the pedigrees of animals in Ireland and Britain appears to have been a matter for their breeders and owners until, in 1791 in England, James Weatherby published *An Introduction to the General Stud Book.* Two years later appeared the first volume of his *General Stud Book.* Weatherby claimed that his publication contained "...a greater mass of authentic information respecting the Pedigrees of Horses than has ever been collected together." Unfortunately these pedigrees were limited to those of race horses and no attempt was made to include details of non-racing, warm or cold-blooded horses. According to Mortimer *et al.* (1978) Weatherby obtained his pedigrees from "...old racing calendars and sales catalogues, information supplied by the breeders of his own day and any private stud books of past breeders that he was able to lay his hands on."

Weatherby's great achievement was not only to record the origins of, but also to define the qualifications for a horse to be considered and accepted as a member of a breed that is now known as the Thoroughbred. Only horses whose pedigrees are recorded in the *General Stud Book* may be considered Thoroughbreds. Weatherby, therefore, perhaps unwittingly, formalised the origin and definition of this breed. Restrictions were later imposed on the qualifications for entry into the *General Stud Book,* partly to protect breeders in Ireland and Britain from imported horses from America and partly to ensure the veracity of pedigrees published in the Book.

All Thoroughbreds whose pedigrees are published in the *General Stud Book* trace back in male line to one of only three ancestors, one of whom, the Byerley Turk, is believed to be a spoil of war taken from the Turkish army at Buda in 1687. This horse was ridden by Colonel Robert Byerley at the Battle of the Boyne in 1690, where Byerley commanded King William's Sixth Dragoon Guards. Subsequently the horse stood at stud in Yorkshire (Walker,1970). Production of Thoroughbreds has resulted from breeding programmes guided by the racing results obtained by the offspring of planned matings which were often based on line and in-breeding. The development of Thoroughbreds coincided with, and resulted in, increased knowledge of how to fix desirable characteristics in livestock The most desirable characteristic in the case of Thoroughbreds was, and remains, that of speed over certain distances.

The value of pedigree knowledge for guiding breeding programmes had been understood long before Weatherby published his book. In the case of foxhounds, for example, the Brocklesby Hunt in England listed pedigrees from 1746 onwards, as did the Belvoir from 1757 and Lord Fitzwilliam's from 1769. It was not until 1841, however, that *The Kennel Stud Book,* recording the pedigree of foxhounds, was first published (Moore, 1981). Nineteen years earlier, in 1822, the pedigrees of Shorthorn Cattle in England had been published in *Coates Shorthorn Herd Book,* which Heath-Agnew

(1983) considered gave Shorthorns "an appearance of uniformity which the breed did not really possess." This statement raises the question of what is a breed?

Plate Thirty: *Scene from The Battle of the Boyne, 1 July 1690, by Theodore Maas, depicting horsemen in action. Colonel Byerley rode his Turk in this famous battle. The speed of the Turk supposedly saved Byerley from being cut-off by King James' men and killed.*

Prepotence and the definition of a breed

Mackay-Smith (1978) has written that "...breeders...consider prepotence essential to any breed of livestock." He defined prepotence as the ability of parents to reproduce themselves as to type, temperament, soundness and performance. Furthermore, Mackay-Smith maintained that "Stallions of the present European warm-blood breeds cannot be relied upon to reproduce themselves solely on the basis of registration in their respective Stud Books - because of mixed ancestry their prepotence is not a breed characteristic, but can only be established for individual stallions through several crops of observable foals." In other words, as far as a practical (though also academic) horseman was concerned, a breed is a group of related animals that, when bred within that group, essentially reproduce their own shared characteristics. Ideally, a stallion of any one breed will be prepotent and convey at least some of the desirable characteristics of that breed to its progeny, regardless of the breed of the mare to which it is put.

Heath-Agnew (1983) has refined the definition of a breed by writing that "...the principle of standardisation" is implicit in a breed. All animals of any one breed must share sufficient common characteristics to be readily identifiable as members of that breed. In the case of Hereford cattle, for instance, John Hewer (1787-1873) bred for many decades from a single line going back to a white-faced bull bred by his father from stock obtained from the

Tomkins and Tully families (who had already attempted to fix certain characteristics, such as white faces, in their cattle by discriminate breeding). The line breeding policy of Hewer and some of his predecessors has produced the hall-mark of the Hereford Cattle breed: their white faces and the fact that "No animal but the white-faced Hereford bull can transmit to all its offspring in the first generation its own particular trade-mark." In 1846 the first volume of the *Hereford Herd Book* was published, as Hereford breeders increasingly realised the necessity of breeding from animals of known parentage and similar conformation, performance and temperament.

Stud books for heavy draught and carriage horses

During the 1870s attempts were made to collect the pedigrees of draught horses in Britain and, to a much lesser extent, in Ireland and to publish Stud Books for the different breeds. In 1877, under the leadership of Herman Biddell, the Suffolk Stud Book Association was founded. In the following year The English Cart Horse Society of Great Britain and

Plate Thirty-one: *One of the most active councillors of The English Cart Horse Society of Great Britain and Ireland was Walter Gilbey (1831-1914), author of twenty-one books and many articles on horse breeding, farming and sporting topics. The Society developed into The Shire Horse Society, of which Gilbey was President in 1883. He was created a Baronet in 1893. Two years later he was President of the Royal Agricultural Society. In 1896 Sir Walter was appointed to the Royal Commission on Horse Breeding in Ireland and thereby played an important role in Irish affairs. In the following year, 1897, Sir Walter was again President of The Shire Horse Society. (From a portrait by W. Q. Orchardson of the first Sir Walter Gilbey Bart. Reproduced by permission of Walter Gilbey, his Grandson)*

Ireland came into being, its cumbersome title being the result of a plea by The Honourable Harry de Vere Pery that "In order to get our foot in Ireland, I think it is very necessary that we should change [the proposed name] to any name at all rather than the English Cart-horse" (Lewis,1979).

The first Stud Book to be published for heavy draught horses in Ireland and Britain was that of the Clydesdale, published in December 1878. On 3 March 1880 Volume I of the *English Cart Horse Stud Book* was published. The first volume of the *Suffolk Horse Stud Book* also appeared in 1880 (Lewis,1979). During the 1880s there was also a move to record the pedigrees of light draught horses in Britain, starting with the foundation of the Cleveland Bay Horse Society in 1883. The first stud book for that Society was published in the following year. Three years later, in 1887, the *Yorkshire Coach Horse Book* appeared.

Horses, population increase and famine

Horses were extremely important in Ireland for agricultural and transport purposes in the early years of the nineteenth century as tillage became increasingly important. Unfortunately, however, the rapid increase in the human population from about four million in 1780 to over eight million in 1845 (Freeman,1965) meant that many of the farms were subdivided into ever smaller plots in order to provide for the essentially rural population.

In 1830 the Royal Dublin Society offered premiums for schemes to divide up land so that there would be allotted "...to the greatest number of cottages a quantity of land of not less than one acre, Irish." This did not necessarily mean that the size of farms, as registered legally, changed greatly, but owners and tenants let and sublet land so that the effective holdings became smaller and smaller in many areas. Much of the let and sublet land was held only in conacre, in other words, on an eleven month lease (Mitchell and Ryan,1998). As the population continued to increase so the cottagers became poorer and poorer and labour became cheap. In many cases it was less expensive to use human labour than that of horses for tillage. Even ploughing could be substituted by digging by hand, increasingly done by teams of spadesmen in the third and fourth decades of the century when labour was plentiful and cheap.

In 1846 the Corn Laws were repealed. They had maintained an artificially high price for grain in order to stimulate production so as to feed the population during the Napoleonic Wars. The Wars themselves had ended in 1815. Repeal heralded a reduction in tillage and hence the need for horses working on the land. In the same and the following two years (1846-48) there was widespread failure of the potato crop in Ireland. Potatoes were the staple food of the poorer elements of the population who consequently suffered from famine and starvation. Within a few years up to one million people died while, within five years of the onset of the Great Famine, another one million people emigrated (Freeman,1965). There was, in consequence, a further reduction in the demand for agricultural produce and for horses working on the land.

Railway mania

During the fateful 1840s Ireland was also affected by railway mania. The first railway in the country, from Dublin to Kingstown (Dun Laoghaire) had opened in 1834. During the 1840s the rail network spread its tentacles through the landscape. By 1853 there were 840 route miles of railway open in Ireland and about seven million passengers were carried that year. By 1872 there were over 2,000 route miles, rising to just over 3,000 route miles in 1894 (Casserley, 1974). The spread of railways ended the need for long

Plate Thirty-two: *Peasant with spade. Digging by hand in the 1820s-40s was often cheaper than ploughing with horses.* (From William Harvey, Original pen and ink sketches of the Irish peasantry circa 1850)

Plate Thirty-three: *A famine funeral in 1847 (Illustrated London News,* 13 February 1847)

distance coach services, such as that from Dublin to Cork, except in isolated areas not yet reached by the rails. Nevertheless it greatly increased the number of people travelling, and many of them needed transport to and from the railway stations. Initially, therefore, the spread of railways was accompanied by an increase in horse-hauled transport.

Plate Thirty-four: *The opening of the Dublin and Kingstown Railway in 1834 heralded a major demand for horse drawn transport to and from stations on the rapidly expanding railway network.* (Source: *lithograph*)

Bianconi, railways and horse-drawn passenger services

Bianconi, the great horse-drawn passenger-vehicle operator, unlike some of his contemporaries, did not oppose the spread of railways. Instead, around 1840 at a meeting of coach and canal boat proprietors who intended to protest against the spread of the steam giants, Bianconi said that "...railways must be made; and I not only do not oppose them, but I have taken shares in the undertakings." Bianconi obviously realised that railways would, at least initially, increase the need for horse transport. By 1843 his vehicles travelled "...no less than 3,800 miles per day", he owned over 1,300 horses and over 100 passenger vehicles varying from four to twenty seaters. His horses consumed from 3,000 to 4,000 tons of hay per annum, and eat between 30,000 and 40, 000 barrels of oats. Even by 1850, when railways were well developed in the country, Bians still covered 3,190 miles per day, although Bianconi had "...switched his cars from the main routes to open new business in outlying districts, providing connections wherever possible with the railways at convenient stations" (Bianconi and Watson,1962). The market for light draught horses of Irish Draught type, which is what Bianconi's horses apparently were, remained relatively buoyant in spite of the Great Famine and the railway mania, certainly until the middle of the nineteenth century.

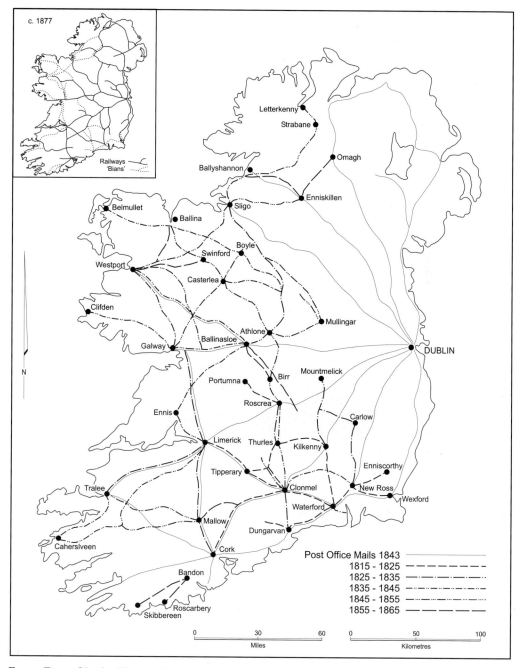

Figure Five: *Charles Bianconi's horse-drawn passenger services, with their dates of operation, and the Post Office Mail services of 1843. Bianconi began his services on 6 July 1815 with a two-wheeled Outside Car (Jaunting Car) pulled between Clonmel and Cahir by 'a sturdy animal bred for hauling artillery limbers... at an average speed of 7.5 miles per hour' (Bianconi and Watson,1962). His enterprise prospered rapidly as he spread his routes throughout much of Ireland. During the 1840s Bianconi owned over 1,300 light draught horses, many of which must have been of Irish Draught type. By the 1870s Bianconi's services were mainly feeders to and from the railways, as the inset map shows. (Redrawn from Freeman,1950)*

Fenians, the Land League and the Land War

In 1858 the Irish Republican Brotherhood, perhaps better known as the Fenian Movement, was founded. In 1867 they rose against the government, but were speedily put down (Moody,1967). The fires of unrest that the Fenians evidenced had earlier flared in the oratory and political objectives of Daniel O'Connell (1775-1847), who was a friend of Bianconi's and who had campaigned for full Catholic emancipation and then for the repeal of the political union of Ireland with Britain and the restoration of the Irish parliament (Whyte,1967). In 1875 the flames were again fanned, by Charles Stewart Parnell, the newly elected Member of Parliament for County Wicklow, in spite of the fact that he was a Protestant landlord with a beautiful estate at Avondale in County Wicklow.

Plate Thirty-five: Daniel O'Connell (1775-1847), friend of Charles Bianconi and the leader of political reform in Ireland in the first half of the nineteenth century.

Parnell committed himself to obstructing the business of Parliament and furthering that of home rule. Four years later, after falling prices, crop failures and exceptionally wet weather had reduced a multitude of small farmers to the edge of bankruptcy, starvation and eviction from their holdings, Parnell became the President of the Irish National Land League (Moody, 1967). Parnell was a gifted leader and skilled politician who was held in high regard by many of the people of Ireland.

The Land League emphasised the rift between landlords and tenants that had festered in Ireland during the nineteenth century. The League campaigned against eviction of tenants from their farms and for a reduction of rents, intending ultimately to transform "...tenant farmers into owners of their own holdings." From 1879-82 "...tenant farmers as a class stood up to the landlords" and the Land War took place.

The Land War was basically a series of agrarian disturbances that challenged the power of landlords who, at that time, controlled much of the land of Ireland. The period

Plate Thirty-six: *Charles Stewart Parnell (1846-1891), the Protestant landlord from Co. Wicklow who became M. P. for that County, President of the Irish National Land League and leader of the Home Rule movement. Parnell's home, Avondale, near Rathdrum, is set in beautifully wooded countryside and the grounds are open to the public.* (Source: O'Shea,1914)

Plate Thirty-seven: *Eviction of a tenant farmer and his family, Vandaleur estate, Co. Clare.* (Photo: The Lawrence Collection, courtesy of the National Library of Ireland)

from then until the end of the century was marked by agrarian unrest and land reform. In 1881 the Land Act diminished landlords' income and, in the next three years, rents fell by an average of almost 20%. This must have militated against the breeding of light draught horses, suitable for agricultural and carriage work, by many of the major landowners. In 1885 the Ashbourne Act established the principle of state-aided land purchase, which was extended by subsequent acts. By the end of the century Ireland had essentially changed from a landlord society into "...a land of peasant owners"(Moody,1967).

Plate Thirty-eight: *In spite of the fall in rents, Colonel Robert Cosby of Stradbally Hall continued to maintain his coach and four in the final decades of the nineteenth century. The Colonel was renowned for his team of liver-coloured chestnuts, 'with every buckle and bow...fresh and perfect and burnished'. There were at least sixteen or seventeen horses in his stable, many of which were hunters. Cosby was a keen whip and drove his coach as far as Pau, in the south of France. The carriage horses included at least one mare that bred a foal that was said to be an Irish Draught. Many Irish Draughts were excellent for carriage work.* (Reproduced by permission of Mr David Cosby)

Political events and their effects on horse breeding

While these great political events were taking place in Ireland it is not surprising that little attention was paid to the formation of stud books, herd books or flock books. Unlike Britain, where prosperity derived from the industrial revolution and its aftermath had shielded landowners from the need to extract as high rents as possible from their estates and had given them sufficient wealth to indulge in the more refined aspects of breeding and pedigree recording, Ireland was at the forefront of agrarian change. Thus it is no surprise that no stud book for Irish Draught Horses or other livestock was established in Ireland in the nineteenth century.

Peasant owners, however misappropriate the term may be for the folk who farmed in Ireland after the breakdown of landlordism, were unlikely to have had sufficient financial resources to breed quality horses, unless assured of a worthwhile return for their enterprise. The latter part of the nineteenth century thus witnessed the erasure of conditions in which, since at least the latter seventeenth century, the production of light draught horses had been fostered. Not only had artificially high prices for agricultural products been removed by the repeal of the Corn Laws, but the spread of railways had led, after an initial rise in the need for light draught horse transport, to a reduction in such transport. Agrarian unrest had caused many landlords to leave the country (although others had been absentee anyway). Even hunting (which had provided a market for some of the more athletic light-draught-type animals) had to be abandoned in some areas during the excesses of the Land League, as in the Ormond and Waterford countries in 1881 and in County Wexford in 1885 (Bowen,1954). Perhaps more important, there was at times a relative fall in produce prices which made various forms of agriculture including tillage, which necessitated the use of light draught horses, at least temporarily uneconomic.

Plate Thirty-nine: *Agrarian unrest, as exemplified by this illustration of a Land League meeting in Kildare in 1881, caused some landlords to leave Ireland and impacted adversely on horse breeding. (*Illustrated London News, *8 January 1881)*

The effect of political unrest and economic decline on horse breeding is shown by the figures for the total horse population of Ireland in 1861, before the Fenian rising and Land League unrest, and before railways were a major threat, and that of 1901. In the former year 475,332 horses were recorded in the country, as opposed to 435,345 in the latter year. More important than the slight decline in numbers was the decline in quality and the export of brood mares. In the three years ending in 1880 just over 9,900 mares were exported. Such landlords as were left in Ireland became alarmed at what they saw as a decline in standards.

Royal Dublin Society premiums for horse breeding

In 1886 the Royal Dublin Society (hereafter referred to as the RDS, or the Society), which was then a mirror of landlord and Ascendancy society, introduced at its annual Horse Show "...prizes for stallions...designed to encourage the judicious breeding of horses by Tenant Farmers in Ireland" (Lewis,1980a). The Ascendancy were "The old land-owning families of Ireland" (Bence-Jones,1987), many of whom were members of the (Anglican) Church of Ireland. They had lost most of their economic and political power as a result of the Land War and the subsequent Land Act of 1881, though some of them had not realised those facts by 1886!

The stallion prizes offered in 1886 were limited to Thoroughbred stallions and the owner of any stallion awarded a prize had to guarantee "...that his horse shall serve in Ireland during the ensuing season, and must guarantee to offer ten subscriptions for the use of *bona fide* tenant farmers' half-bred mares not exceeding four years old" (Lewis,1980a).

In 1887 the Society offered sixteen Service Premiums to Thoroughbred stallions "...suitable for getting Hunters and other Half-bred Horses" on condition that each Premium sire served "...if required, not less than fifty Half-bred Mares, the *bona fide* property of Farmers." Finance for these premiums came from "Her Majesty's Government [which had] promised [to encourage] improvement in the Breed of Horses and cattle in Ireland."

For many years the RDS had, in some ways, acted on behalf of the government in Ireland. By 1886 it had become obvious, at least to the Prime Minister of the United Kingdom, W. E. Gladstone, that peace and prosperity in Ireland could only be attained if the country was granted home rule. (In 1800 an Act for the legislative union of Ireland with Great Britain had been passed by the Irish and British parliaments. The union of Great Britain and Ireland had taken place in 1801, with Parliament thereafter sitting at Westminster in London). Home rule would necessitate the foundation of a variety of government departments, such as a Department of Agriculture.

In 1886 Gladstone introduced his Home Rule Bill into Parliament in London, but the Bill was defeated. Until such time as it, or a similar Bill was enacted, and Ireland became internally self-governing, why not use the RDS as a sort of nascent Department of Agriculture? That seems to have been the thinking behind granting the Society money to improve "...the Breed of Horses and cattle in Ireland."

In 1887 the Society divided Ireland into sixteen Premium Stallion Districts for the breeding season of 1888 and then appointed a Local Committee in each District to select mares for service by the Premium Stallion allocated to the District. In most Districts there was intense competition for nominations and, on average, there were 109 mares inspected per District although only fifty nominations were on offer. In the Portadown District, in the north of Ireland, 258 mares competed for nominations, while 168 did so in the Ballymote District in County Sligo and 143 in Dunmanway in west Cork. There was thus no shortage of Half-bred mares in Ireland in 1888, although no evidence appears to exist to indicate how many of them were Irish Draught in type. Half-breds were the progeny of a Thoroughbred sire on a non-Thoroughbred but warm blood mare, which may well have been an Irish Draught, even though that name had yet to be given to Ireland's distinctive light draught horses.

For the next ten years the RDS continued to offer Service Premiums to Thoroughbred stallions and to award nominations to Half-bred mares. The Society also introduced veterinary examinations to ensure that stallions were free of hereditary diseases that constituted unsoundness. The Society also insisted on evidence that stallions

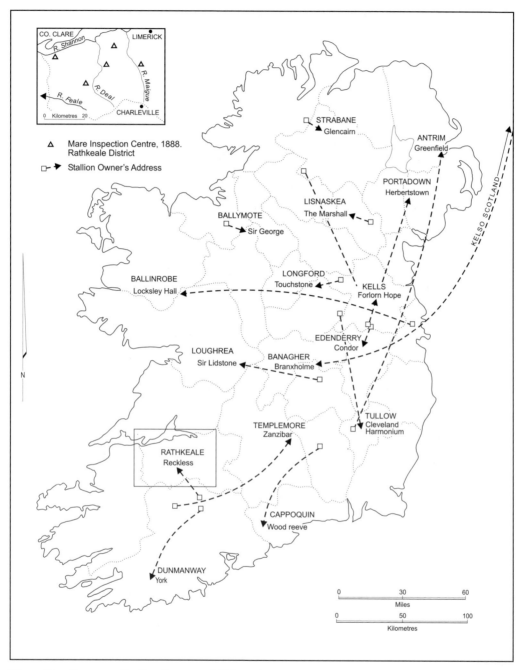

Figure Six: *Premium Stallion Districts, 1888 stud season. The name of the stallion allocated to each District is shown, as is its owner's address. The mare inspection centres for the Rathkeale District are shown as an inset.* (Redrawn from Lewis,1980a)

already standing at stud were fertile and, from 1892, published an annual *Register of Approved Stallions,* all of which were Thoroughbreds. Nevertheless, as the years went by it became increasingly obvious that there was need for a comprehensive enquiry into horse breeding in Ireland.

Plate Forty: *W. E. Gladstone introducing his Home Rule Bill in the House of Commons, 8 April 1886. The Bill was defeated. (Illustrated London News,* 17 April 1886)

The Royal Commission on Horse Breeding

In 1896 a Royal Commission was appointed to enquire into the breeding of horses in Ireland. The Commission was Chaired by the Earl of Dunraven, who lived in Adare in County Limerick and owned a number of stallions that were registered by the RDS. Other Commissioners were Frederick Wrench, who was a member of the Society's Stallion Registration Committee, a member of the Congested Districts Board and a former President of the Hackney Society; the Earl of Enniskillen, who had an estate of "...30,000 acres of heavy soil in an area that had imported Clydesdales to work it during the eighteenth-century expansion in corn production" (Fell,1991); Sir Walter Gilbey, who was one of the leading equestrian writers of the period and a wealthy man, Master of the Old Berkshire Hunt in England, a former President of the Shire Horse Society (1883) and a great supporter of Hackney horses; Percy La Touche, the Irish banker and County Wicklow landowner and member of the Stallion Registration Committee of the RDS; Lord Ashtown and Lord Rathdonnell, both of whom were members of the RDS Stallion Registration Committee; the Marquis of Londonderry, a major landowner, formerly Lord Lieutenant of Ireland (1886-9), and who had just ended his term of office as President of the Clydesdale Stud Book Society; R. G. Carden, a member of the Carden family who were major landowners in County Tipperary and who was a major authority on hunters and, from 1898, was to become a member of the Stallion Registration Committee of the RDS; Thomas Grattan Esmonde, a member of an influential Wexford family of Ballynastragh, Gorey, (this castellated mansion,

Plate Forty-one: *The Fourth Earl of Dunraven (1841-1926), of Adare, Co. Limerick. Dunraven was a Knight of St Patrick, Under Secretary for the Colonies (1885-7), a Privy Councillor and chaired the Commission of Inquiry into the horse breeding industry. In 1897, together with other members of the Commission, he submitted an important report. Dunraven was the owner of the Fort Union Stud. Among his Thoroughbred stallions was Atratus, advertised at a fee of £5 for Thoroughbred mares, £3 for Half-bred mares, '...Owner's Tenants' mares, £2.' The Dunravens were descended from the Quins of Inchiquin, in Co. Clare, and according to Burke (1939) are 'one of the few families of Celtic origin in the Irish peerage'. (Photo: History of the Turf)*

Plate Forty-two: *The 6th Marquis of Londonderry, K. G., P. C., G. C. V. O., C. B. (1852-1919), Lord Lieutenant of Ireland 1886-89 and a member of the Royal Commission on Horse Breeding.* (Source: Apperley, 1926)

which overlooked a scenic lake, was burnt in 1923); Henry Fitzwilliam; T. A. St Quintin; and J. L. Carew, whose family owned almost 18,000 acres in County Wexford and more elsewhere in Ireland and whose seat was the magnificent Classical-style mansion of Castleborough, Enniscorthy, that was subsequently to be burnt in 1923. These gentlemen were essentially drawn from the landowning and Ascendancy society of Ireland and were representative of Anglo-Irish rather than Irish society.

Frederick Wrench was a great supporter of Hackney horses and believed that Hackney stallions would do much to improve the quality of horses in the Congested Districts. The Congested Districts Board had been established in 1891 to cater for the needs of those poverty stricken areas of Ireland where the rateable valuation was less than £1-10s per head. In order to improve farming in those areas the Board placed stallions ranging from jack-asses to Thoroughbreds at strategic locations in order to serve mares at low or even non-existent fees.

By 1896 the Board owned thirty-six Hackney stallions and they served many mares in the poor areas of Connemara, west Mayo, parts of Roscommon and Sligo, much of Donegal and parts of west Kerry and the extreme west of Cork. The interests of the Hackney were well represented on the Board of the Royal Commission, some of whose members felt that Hackney blood was essential if quality horses suitable for light draught and army purposes were to be produced in Ireland in future.

Other members of the Board were strong supporters of heavy draught horses, especially Clydesdales, while the majority was interested in the production of quality hunters and army remounts produced mainly by crossing Thoroughbred sires on half-bred, farmers' mares.

Plate Forty-three: *Frederick Wrench, J. P., who served on the Royal Commission on Horse Breeding, and was a former President of the Hackney Society, a member of the Congested Districts Board, the Stallion Registration Committee of the Royal Dublin Society and subsequently a member of the committee on horse breeding of the Department of Agriculture. (Photo: courtesy of The Royal Dublin Society)*

Evidence: the existence of Irish Draught Horses

During the meetings of the Royal Commission evidence was heard from many horse dealers, breeders and others interested in horse production in Ireland. Among them were people like Colonel de Robeck, from County Kildare, who said that in his area: "One man has what they call an Irish cart horse. He has very little hair on his legs, is a very strong horse and looks like a cross of the Clydesdale. [Another man has] what he calls an Irish cart horse,...a good useful stamp of horse to get a tram horse or canal horse, but it is not a very hairy-legged horse."

Plate Forty-four: *Colonel H. de Robeck (1859-1929) from Co. Kildare, who described 'an Irish cart horse' to the Commissioners. The Baron de Robeck was Master of the Kildare Foxhounds from 1897-1906, an expert horseman and a renowned point-to-point rider. (Photo: Dublin Horse Show Magazine)*

Richard Flynn, from Tulsk in County Roscommon, introduced the term Irish Draught to the Commissioners: "The Irish draught was a breed in itself, I think; they were a sort of slow hunter with clean hard legs....they could jump well and gallop fairly fast and were never tired; they were a real genuine Irish breed."

Plate Forty-five: *An Irish Draught of Colonel de Robeck's period:* **Discovery (19)**, *16.1 hands. foaled in 1902 and sired by* **Ruglaw**. (Source: *Irish Draught Horse Book*)

Major C. W. Studdart of Corofin in County Clare , who had judged at the Hunters' Improvement Society's show in England in 1888 (MacGregor-Morris, 1986), was even more informative: "...an old Irish mare is a long, low mare, about 15.2, with good neck, head and shoulders. She might have some hair on her legs, too....she can go eight Irish miles twice a day for...a creel of turf and come back none the worse for it. She trots...five or six miles an hour. They are produced from old Irish blood, with some crosses of Thoroughbred blood."

Report of the Commission

When the Commissioners finally reported in 1897 they wrote that "...the number of horses now exported [from Ireland] is nearly 40,000 annually." Perhaps they should have added that over 300 000 horses were then employed in London alone, few of them surviving for more than six or seven years in the terrible conditions of that city, and that many of them were bred in Ireland (Gordon, 1893). The commissioners divided on their recommendations, but Dunraven wrote that the South of Ireland "...was the chief mart in the world for high class horses for both riding and driving purposes. These horses are almost entirely the produce of thoroughbred sires, or of half-bred sires of the hunter type." Dunraven and his supporters added that Thoroughbred and certain Half-bred sires should be used for breeding and recommended that if they were registered they should first be vetted for soundness. Furthermore, "...the Hackney is not, in our opinion, a desirable sire." Finally, "...as the main industry in Ireland consists in the breeding of a lighter class of horse, and a large proportion of the land is not adapted to the heavy draught horse, we consider that the supply of such stallions may ...be left to private enterprise", but that State aid should be given for the production of "...hunters, high class carriage horses, and remounts."

Plate Forty-six: *Lord Enniskillen (1845-1924), instigator of a minority report published by the Commission of Inquiry into the Horse Breeding Industry. Enniskillen was a Knight of St Patrick, Deputy Lieutenant of Co. Fermanagh, Justice of the Peace, and had been Member of Parliament for Enniskillen (1880-5) before succeeding as 4th Earl (Burke,1939)* (Photo: courtesy of The Royal Dublin Society)

Lord Enniskillen and his supporters thought differently. They stated that the majority of horses in Ireland were used for agricultural purposes: 89% in Connaught, 88% in Ulster, 85% in Munster and 74% in Leinster. The RDS *Register* included none of the agricultural stallions, of which there were at least 816 in Ireland in 1896, neither did it include any other than Thoroughbred sires, even though there were 651 Half-bred stallions in the country (these statistics had been collected by the police). The Enniskillen faction concluded that "...the needs of each class of breeder should be recognised", thinking that it was essential to register Thoroughbred, Hunter, Cart Horse and Hackney stallions. The scene was thus set, ready for the dawn of a new century, for the establishment of a new Register of Stallions and, possibly, a new policy on horse breeding.

Chapter Six

THE TWENTIETH CENTURY:
RECOGNITION AND REGISTRATION OF THE IRISH DRAUGHT HORSE

The dawn of a new century and the administration of agriculture

The twentieth century began with major reorganisation of the ways in which government was involved in the development and administration of agriculture in Ireland. In May 1900 the first meeting of the Council of Agriculture was held, in Dublin. This was the body newly established by the government to take charge of agriculture in Ireland. In his opening address the Chairman, the Right Honourable Horace Plunkett, M. P.,.P. C., who had already made a great reputation for himself by his work for the Irish creamery movement, stated that "We ought to watch very carefully the requirements of the War Office as regards remounts....It is already in contemplation by the Department to constitute a Committee...to deal with this important question of horse-breeding."

The Department's Register of Stallions

In 1901 the Department of Agriculture and Technical Instruction for Ireland issued its own *Register of Stallions* and this included Clydesdales and Shires as well as Thoroughbreds. Thenceforth there was no need for the RDS *Register*, nor for the Society's premiums for stallions, although some money still existed in the Society's coffers for the award of premiums. The last of this money was disbursed in 1903, when the final ten premiums for Thoroughbred stallions were awarded. In 1901 the Society had broken with tradition and among the twenty eight stallion premiums that were awarded were three for "Agricultural Stallions", at least two of which were Clydesdales (Lewis, 1980a).

Although the establishment of the Department of Agriculture's stallion register was generally welcomed, fears were expressed that the registration of heavy draught sires throughout the country might damage the quality of Irish horses, which were active light draught-type hunters suitable for the carriage and remount trade rather than slow heavy draught beasts.

Among the opponents of geographically indiscriminate Clydesdale and Shire registration was Patrick J. Hanlon from Grangeforth in County Carlow, an outspoken member of the Council of Agriculture. In 1904, partly as a result of lobbying by Hanlon, the Department decided "...that no new sires of the Clydesdale and Shire breeds should be registered except for the province of Ulster, the counties of Dublin and Louth, and the district comprised within a radius of ten miles of the city of Cork. The object...was to check the great impetus that had been given to the importation of Clydesdales and Shires; for most authorities agree that such sires, if too freely imported, will impair the reputation of Irish horses" (AGR,1903-4).

Irish Draught stallions

In 1905 the Department made a momentous decision, and "...offered to owners of stallions of the old Irish Draught type and of half-bred stallions of the Hunter-type, a premium of £50 for selected stallions" (AGR,1904-5). Twelve such stallions were approved and subsidised. For the first time, in an official document, recognition had been given to the Irish Draught, although it was not until 1911 that Irish Draughts were given formal recognition by the listing of stallions under that designation in the Department's Register. Thirteen stallions were registered as Irish Draughts in 1911 and the same number in the following year. In 1913 and 1924 numbers fell to a dozen, but rose again to thirteen in 1915. No Irish Draughts were listed during the height of the First World War, in 1916 or 1917, but there was a steady increase in registrations from 1918 until 1921 (immediately preceding the political partition of Ireland), from 44 in 1918 to 60 in 1921 (Lewis,1979).

Irish Draught mares

In 1911, in addition to stallion inspections, the owners of mares were invited to submit them for inspection for registration as Irish Draughts. Out of 5,040 mares that were subsequently inspected, only 264 were judged suitable for registration. Thus, through the official government horse breeding schemes, suitable mares as well as stallions were formally accepted as Irish Draughts.

Artillery horses

In 1915, during the 1914-18 (First World) War, Lord Selbourne, President of the Board of Agriculture and Fisheries in Britain, appointed a Committee to advise on the supply of horses for military purposes. The Committee reported that: "We consider the encouragement of the breeding of horses suitable for artillery and light draught to be of the utmost national importance....This type of horse [is] from 1200 to 1400 lbs., from 15.2 to 15.3 hands, on short clean legs, with deep, well-placed shoulders, short back and quick balanced action..." This was essentially a description of the Irish Draught Horse or, as Lord Derby put it: "... a carthorse that will trot". To further the breeding of horses suitable for military use the Government (of what was then the United Kingdom that included the whole of Ireland as well as Britain) bought Colonel Hall Walker's stud at Tully, Kildare. The stud was taken over on 1 January 1916 (MacGregor-Morris, 1986). Although Tully specialised in Thoroughbreds, the Board's encouragement of light draught horse breeding undoubtedly influenced the Department of Agriculture in Ireland in its efforts to develop the Irish Draught.

Irish Draught Horse Book and the establishment of a breed

In 1918 the Department of Agriculture published Volume One of the *Irish Draught Horse Book*, which listed stallions and mares. Unfortunately none of the 264 mares passed in 1911 were included in the volume. In 1919, when the second volume of the *Irish Draught Horse Book* was published, it contained the statement that the Department believed that "A lesson may be learned from the manner in which the various English breeds of live stock have been improved within recent years through the establishment of stud books and the formation of breed societies." The Department intended that the Irish Draught stud book should be kept open for a "limited number of years; at the expiration of that period...none but the qualified progeny of registered mares and sires will be eligible for entry". In other words, by careful selection of foundation stock and by examination of progeny, the Department intended that the Irish Draught should be formally established as a breed.

Carden's description of Irish Draughts

Although stallions were registered by the Department of Agriculture as Irish Draughts from 1911 (with the exception of some years, as already noted), there was at that time no stated standard for the breed, or type. In 1907 R. G. Carden wrote that prior to about the year 1850 there was a breed of horses known as the Irish cart or draught horse: "It must not be taken that the words "cart" and "draught" imply that these animals were purely kept for agricultural purposes, or were in any way of the same type or blood as what are known in England and Scotland at the present day as the Shire and Clydesdale, as there are many

Plate Forty-seven: *R. G. Carden, D. L., J. P. (1866-1916) of Fishmoyne, Templemore in Co. Tipperary, who was a member of the Royal Commission on Horse Breeding in Ireland, a member of the stallion registration committee of the Royal Dublin Society and a well-known stallion owner and horse breeder. In 1907 Carden published the first appreciable description of Irish Draughts. John Rutter Carden, his cousin, 'was known as "Woodcock" because he was so often shot at by his tenants' (Burke,1976). (Photo: Dublin Horse Show Magazine)*

instances in which some of these "Irish draught horses" proved to be the best hunters of their time."

Carden wrote of Irish Draughts as "...a long, low build of animal, rarely exceeding 15.3 or 16 hands high, with strong, short, clean legs, plenty of bone and substance, short backs, strong loins and quarters...slightly upright shoulders, strong necks and a smallish head. They had good, straight, level action, without its being extravagant, could trot, canter and gallop. They were also excellent jumpers....No authentic information in regard to their breeding is now available, though, no doubt, many breeders carefully preserved the strain in their breeding studs for many years, but it may generally be taken that the original breeding of the "Irish draught horse" was the result of the cross of the imported thoroughbred sires on the stronger of the well-bred mares of the country, which latter must have had an infusion of Spanish or Arabian blood in their veins" (Carden, 1907).

Whether horses of the type described by Carden were confined to Ireland is debatable. In 1912 A. W. Anstruther, in presenting a report of the Board of Agriculture and Fisheries in Britain, referred to "...the old breed of Welsh Light Cart Horses", which provided "...light legged mares suitable for Hunter breeding". The Board had initiated a scheme "...to preserve the native hardy breed and ensure its reproduction" (Hunter Stud Book, VI; Lewis,1983), but the scheme did not succeed. Another breed, or type, of light draught horses that also disappeared in the early years of the twentieth century was the Devon pack horse: the Irish Draught was lucky to survive.

Inspection tours and the selection of mares

Over 7,000 mares were examined by the official inspectors of the Department of Agriculture in their tours of 1917-1919 and, of these, 688 were accepted for registration as Irish Draughts. Details of 678 of these mares were subsequently published in Volumes I-III of the *Irish Draught Horse Book*, although it is not known why details of the other ten were omitted; perhaps they died before publication. The *Books* usually record the name and official registration number of the mare, the name and address of its owner and, occasionally, of its breeder, the mare's colour, distinguishing marks, height, year of birth and, in most cases, limited information as to its pedigree. In a very few cases the foals produced by the mare, with the names of their sires, are listed. Two further volumes of the *Book* were published, in 1921 and, after the partition of Ireland, in 1932. Another volume appears to have been almost ready for publication on the outbreak of the Second World War, in 1939, but never appeared.

The three inspectors in 1917: James Clarke of Navan; Patrick Shelly of Callan in County Kilkenny; and P. J. Howard, M. R. C. V. S. of Ennis in County Clare; reported that:

"In making our selections of mares we adopted a good average standard of merit, and were particularly careful to exclude mares showing coarseness or signs of imported cart-horse blood. No well-made mare that could be regarded as a good, useful farm animal of the clean legged draught type was passed over without careful consideration. With regard to the stallions, in making our selections we set a high standard of merit, and we have not recommended for entry any sires respecting which there was a reasonable doubt in our minds, either on the score of general merit, or in the matter of pedigree. Our main concern was to choose animals having, in the first place, a good general conformation; and secondly, true Irish Draught character and weight. In considering the question of breeding, we have been most careful to exclude such sires as had imported cart-horse

strains so far as we could trace. We were not so strict in regard to thoroughbred blood, and we have recommended a few sires which have one or two crosses of Thoroughbred more or less remote in their pedigree. With these exceptions the selected sires come from old strains of Irish Draught horses.

The question of action also received considerable attention, and whilst we did not look for anything in the nature of extravagant action, we satisfied ourselves that the horses we selected were reasonably straight and true movers."

The distribution of mares

The distribution of mares registered in the first three volumes of the *Irish Draught Horse Book* was mapped by Lewis (1980b). None were located in the boggy lands of Erris or in Connemara, nor in those of Iveragh and the rocky and boggy peninsulas south of Kenmare, except in the fertile lands at Bantry and along the south coast to Goleen. The uplands of the Wicklow Mountains, the Comeraghs and Knockmealdowns and other uplands in the south of Ireland were also devoid of Irish Draughts. There were very few in Ulster (including Donegal), Louth and County Dublin, which were all heavy draught horse areas. The relatively rich lands extending inland past Ennis from the Fergus estuary in County Clare were Irish Draught areas, as were the coastlands along the northern shore of the River Shannon west of the Fergus estuary and the Loop Head peninsula, but the rugged limestone lands of the Burren were not suited to them and they were absent there.

The size of mares

The smallest mares registered in the first three volumes of the *Irish Draught Horse Book* were 15 hands high, the tallest were of 16.2 hands. 86% of the mares were between 15.2 and 16 hands and 40% were of 15.3 hands. The typical Irish Draught mare was therefore of 15.2 or 15.3 hands. Analysis of mare height spatially shows, however, that mares were larger in some areas of Ireland and smaller in others. The tallest mares, averaged over unit areas of 100 square miles in which there were eight or more mares per area, existed in south and east County Wexford and in County Down. The smallest mares, analysed similarly, existed in the disadvantaged terrain of County Mayo and adjacent areas, where the drumlin landscape of little fields and heavy and generally ill-drained soils probably militated against the development of larger animals. Irish Draughts thus seem to have been adjusted to local conditions, at least as far as height was concerned, in the early part of the twentieth century (Lewis,1980b,1981). Whether they were similarly adjusted in earlier times is now a matter for conjecture. Since only nine mares out of the total of 673 for which data exists were just 15 hands high, it is likely that smaller mares were not accepted by the Inspectors for registration.

Irish Draught stallions in 1921

The Department's *Register of Stallions* for 1921 records not only the names of Irish Draught stallions, but gives some information about them and about the places where, during 1921, they were to stand at stud. The names of the owners and their addresses are also given. The registered stallions were concentrated south of a line from the Boyne to Galway Bay. There was no registered Irish Draught stallion standing at stud in what was to become Northern Ireland, and only a handful existed north of a line from Dublin to Galway (Lewis,1979).

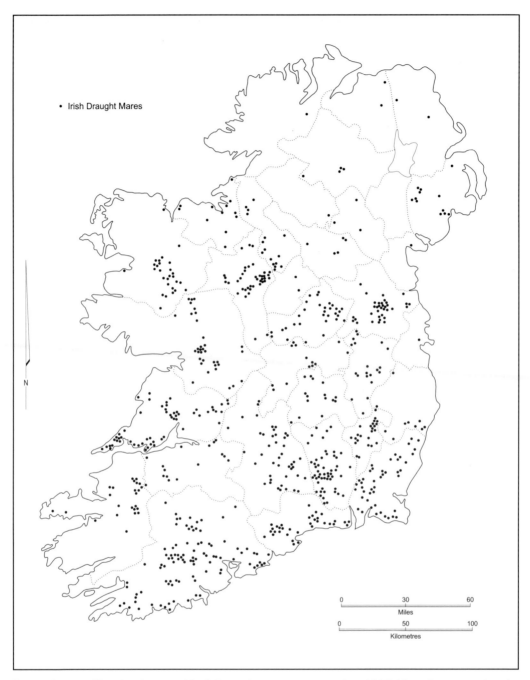

Figure Seven: *The distribution of Irish Draught mares inspected in 1917-19 and registered in the first three volumes of the Irish Draught Horse Book.* (Redrawn after Lewis, 1980b)

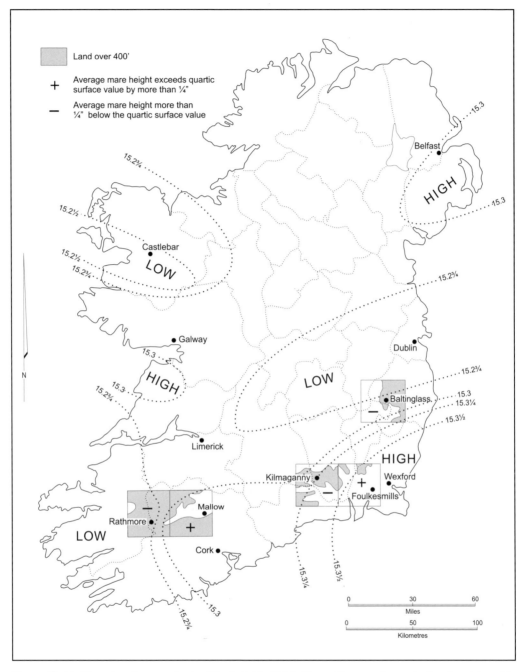

Figure Eight: *Trend surface analysis of the height of Irish Draught mares inspected and registered in 1917-19 and included in the first three volumes of the Irish Draught Horse Book. Mares were smaller, on average, in the Clew Bay region of Mayo and in the west of Cork and Kerry than in the more fertile areas further east. They were also smaller in upland areas than in adjacent lowlands, as around Rathmore and Kilmaganny. (Redrawn after Lewis,1980b)*

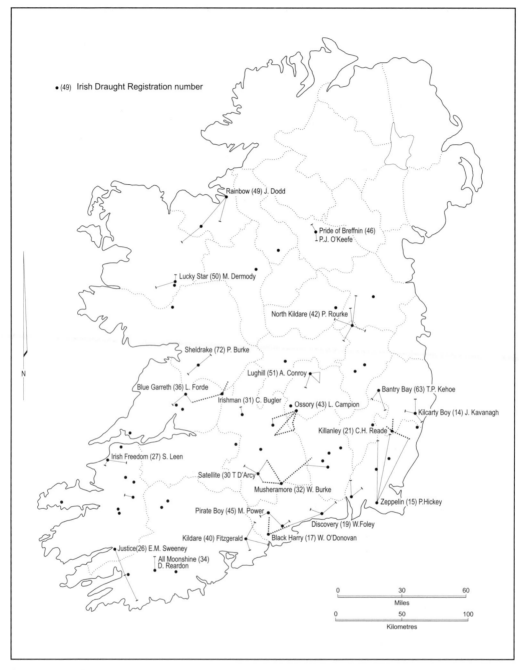

Figure Nine: *Registered Irish Draught stallions at stud in 1921. Lines connect points at which each stallion stood at stud, exact routes were not recorded. The names and registered numbers of stallions that travelled appreciable distances, and the names of their owners, are shown.* (Redrawn from Lewis, 1979)

One of the horses that travelled furthest for his mares was **Rainbow (49)**, owned by James Dodd, who was a well known veterinary surgeon in Sligo. Dodd's horse was a 16 hand bay, foaled in 1915, by **Starlight (7)** out of **Lady Dolly. Starlight (7)** was a 16.2 hand bay horse foaled in 1904, by **Comet (1)** by an unregistered sire of the same name. The dam of **Comet (1)** was by **Vanderhum**, a Thoroughbred stallion that had first been listed in the RDS *Register of Thoroughbred Stallions* in 1892 when he belonged to Kevin Mullins, a farmer and stallion man from Glenmore in County Kilkenny. There was thus a strong infusion of Thoroughbred blood in **Rainbow (49)** and it was such infusions that caused many people to consider the Irish Draught as a type, rather than a breed

County Kerry had more registered Irish Draught stallions in 1921 than any other county: nine, although only two of them travelled appreciable distances for their mares. **Justice (26)**, owned by Edmond M'Sweeney of Gerahduveen, Kenmare, travelled to Kenmare on Wednesdays, Bantry (in County Cork) on Fridays, and Skibbereen (also in County Cork) on Saturdays. **Justice (26)** had been foaled in 1911 and stood 15.3 hands, was grey and was by **Young J P (12)**, who also stood 15.3 hands and was grey, like *his* unregistered father: **Young Sir Henry.** The names Sir Henry, Young Sir Henry and Old Sir Henry were favourites among breeders in west Cork and adjacent Kerry and it is by no means certain as to which was really which! The registered **Young Sir Henry (11)** was foaled in 1901.

One of the most important stallions listed in 1921 was **Kildare (40)**, who stood with Mrs Fitzgerald in the east Cork- west Waterford area. Mrs Fitzgerald lived at Clonmult, in the hills between Midleton and Tallow. She was a renowned stallion owner, standing a Thoroughbred named **Mount Edgar** in addition to her Irish Draught sire.

Plate Forty-eight: *Kildare (40), a grey horse of 16.1 hands, foaled in 1913 and by* **Young J. P. (12)** *out of* **Molly Grey (321)**. *This was one of the most influential of all Irish Draught sires. (Source: Irish Draught Horse Book)*

Kildare (40) was a grey horse of 16.1 hands, foaled in 1913 and bred by Thomas O'Donnell of Buttevant. Kildare (40) was by Young J P (12), who was foaled in 1891 and was bred by C. Blackmore at Killenaule in County Tipperary. The dam of Kildare (40) was Molly Grey (321) by Young Arthur II (10), a sire who stood 16.1 hands, was foaled in 1895, was grey and was by the unregistered sire Home Rule. This latter horse was by one of the best known Hunter sires in the south of Ireland, Garrett, who was mentioned in the Report of the Royal Commission in 1897 as a Draught (Fell,1991). Molly Grey (321) was grey, 16 hands high, foaled in 1905 and bred by Timothy O'Sullivan at Killinardrish in County Cork.

Plate Forty-nine: *Molly Grey (321)*, *foaled in 1905, the 16.0 hands grey dam of* *Kildare (40)*. *She was a prize winner at Cork Show in 1918.* (Source: *Irish Draught Horse Book*)

Kildare (40) is one of the most influential Irish Draught sires. Fell (1991) has written that he is one of "...the two most important Irish Draught stallions since the start of formal registration." Kildare (40) was the sire of 22 registered stallions. Among his progeny was Pride of Cork (88), who sired another 17 stallions.

In 1921 Kildare (40) travelled the area between Midleton, Youghal and Tallow in order to service mares. Three years later, in 1924, Kildare (40) was sold to the Larkins family of Woodlands, Killimer, in County Galway. While there the stallion was taken to serve mares during the breeding season at Loughreagh on Thursdays, Athenry on Fridays, Ballinasloe on Saturdays and home that night and all day Sunday, Borrisokane on Mondays and at home on Tuesdays and Wednesdays. All these journeys were done by train (Fell,1991).

Denis Vaughan has pointed out that in the 1920s and 1930s "...the extensive train service helped farmers to be scientific in their breeding policies. People and stock could attend markets, fairs, race meetings and so on, with schedules arranged to fit in and running costs subsidised by the Government." The County Galway owners of Kildare (40) certainly made good use of train services, to the great benefit of Irish Draught Horse breeding in east Galway (Fell,1991).

Vaughan has also stated that at the same period "The main use ...for Draughts was road work, taking a fair load at a good speed, which caused them to evolve into a nice type of carriage horse" (Fell,1991). In fact, as has already been shown, Irish Draughts had fulfilled the role of carriage horse for at least 200 years before then, but Vaughan's comments confirm that, even in the early twentieth century, Irish Draughts were regarded as carriage horses as well as workers on the land and as horses that could be ridden and would hunt.

Licensing of all stallions

The licensing of all stallions in Ireland, including Irish Draughts, became mandatory in 1920. During that year there were 2,105 applications for licences of which 1,718 were granted. 159 of these licences were for one year only because "...the horses were unsound or...unsuitable, but...for various reasons [the] Department considered it inadvisable to refuse Licences." The political partition of Ireland in 1922 resulted in licensing of stallions in what then became Northern Ireland being taken over by the Northern Ministry of Agriculture. In that and the following year "The disturbed state of the country operated against rigid enforcement of [licensing], and it is feared that in some cases unlicensed horses were used for stud purposes"(AGR,1921-2). As far as the Department of Agriculture in the newly independent Twenty Six Counties was concerned, however, "There is...every reason to hope that it will be possible to take steps to ensure that no stallion will be serving without a licence during the 1924 service season" (AGR,1922-3).

Conditions in Ireland in 1922-3 are reflected by statements in the *Annual General Report* of the Department of Agriculture for those years. "The period covered by this Report corresponds generally to the year beginning with the 1st October, 1922, and ending on 30th September, 1923.It was a year of anxiety and struggle. The post-war depression...continued to weigh down Irish agriculture....During the greater portion of the time large areas of the country were in a disturbed condition. Railway and other travelling and transit facilities were frequently interrupted and in some cases suspended for considerable periods." Under those conditions it was remarkable that efforts were maintained to ensure that stallions were registered and no surprise that publication of Volume V of the *Irish Draught Horse Book* did not take place in 1922.

Between 1924 and 1926 it appears that no register of stallions was produced. The grand total of registered stallions printed for that period in the *General Reports* of the Minister of Agriculture of what was the Twenty Six Counties included "...stallions entered in the Irish Draught Horse book", suggestive of the difficulties of proper administration and of the need for cosmetic statistics in the official returns.

Commission of Inquiry into the Horse Breeding Industry

During the early 1930s there was considerable concern about the state of horse breeding in Ireland. A Commission of Inquiry was established and reported in 1935 that "many of what are called Irish Draught horses at present are not of the correct type. Many ...are too light and leggy." The Commission recommended careful selection in future with an emphasis on constant grading up. The rapid spread of motor vehicles and the outbreak of the Second World War, however, probably had more important effects on the development of the Irish Draught than did the recommendations of the Commission.

Irish Draught stallions in 1939

The *Register of Stallions* for 1939, immediately preceding the outbreak of the Second World War, provides sufficient information to map the distribution of registered Irish Draught stallions and to show the routes they followed in search of trade, of mares to serve. The pattern of distribution of Irish Draught sires was markedly different from that of 1921 (Lewis,1979). Virtually no Irish Draughts travelled in east Cork-west Waterford, although they remained popular in west Cork and in Kerry. Further north they concentrated in a great belt extending westwards from Arklow, through south Wicklow, across Carlow, north Kilkenny, central and north Tipperary, and across Clare to the shores of the Atlantic Ocean. From the Clare-north Tipperary area a secondary concentration extended north through the fertile lands of east Galway and into the Plains of Mayo. A subsidiary concentration existed extending from the Killala area of north Mayo eastwards to the western edge of Longford.

Although there had been a number of Irish Draught stallions that travelled appreciable distances for their mares in 1921, the networks of travelling stallions were far better developed in 1939. Some, like Richard Barton's **Irish Champion (87),** almost

Plate Fifty: *Irish Guard (13), the grandsire of Carrigeen Lad (123), was a 16.05 hands bay, bred by John Kavanagh and foaled in 1912, by Prince Henry (5) out of a mare by the unregistered Irishman. Irish Guard (13) sired six registered Irish Draught stallions and has had an important influence on the breed. The photograph was taken when the horse was twelve years old and portrays the stallion as a powerful, alert and clean-legged animal, with excellent shoulders and deep girth. He would have made a fine carriage horse or weight carrying hunter. Like many Irish Draughts his croup tends to fall away. The knee guards suggest that Irish Guard (13) had been boxed, probably by rail, to where he was photographed.* (Source: Irish Draught Horse Book)

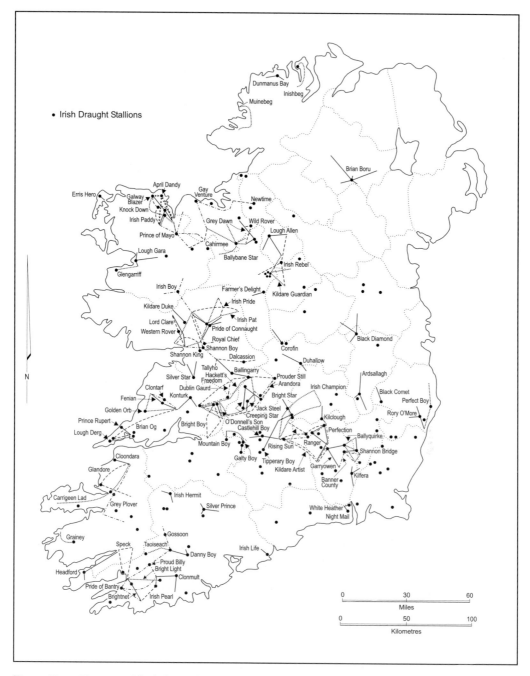

Figure Ten: *Registered Irish Draught stallions standing at stud in 1939. Lines connect locations to which stallions travelled regularly to serve mares. Single dots, with no radiating lines, represent stallions that apparently did not travel for their mares. The increase in the number of stallions since 1921 was remarkable.* (Redrawn from Lewis,1979)

certainly travelled at least some of their route by train. Even J. Dillon's **Carrigeen Lad (123)** may have used the rails, for the Dingle light railway led almost from his home stable in Tralee all the way to Dingle town, with convenient stops at stations such as Anascaul along the route. This 16 hand bay horse had been foaled in 1925 and was by the 16.0 1/2 hand bay horse **Irish Mail (60)** who was, in turn, the son of the same size and colour sire; **Irish Guard (13)**. That horse was by the 16.1 hands grey **Prince Henry (5),** who was by the unregistered **King Henry** by the equally unregistered **Sir Henry** and his father, **'Old Sir Henry'.**

By 1939 the farming community had come to rely almost entirely upon the Irish Draught for motive power. Truly heavy horses, such as Clydesdales and Shires, were only needed in the major areas of tillage where the soils were of sticky heavy clays, as in parts of Counties Dublin and Louth and in much of Ulster. They were also needed for traction in the major cities of Dublin and Cork. Elsewhere the need was for a horse that could cope with mainly light farm work, with only a limited amount of ploughing, that could trot with the trap to market, and that could take its master hunting when the chance arose. The horse that filled this role was the Irish Draught.

MacLysaght wrote in 1939 that: "Nowadays a good ploughman, with a pair of lively Irish Draught horses, will plough nearly a statute acre in a day - a matter for surprise to farmers accustomed to the heavy, slow-moving Shires and Clydesdales of England and Scotland."

The Second World War

The Irish Draught increased in popularity during the difficult days of the Second World War (1939-44), when petrol and diesel were in very short supply, new motor vehicles were almost impossible to obtain and spare parts for vehicles were a rarity. In July 1942 the Emergency Powers (Control of Export) Order came into effect in what is now, *de facto*, the Republic of Ireland (hereafter referred to as RI or as the Republic), prohibiting the export of horses except under licence. During 1942 "Licences were only issued for the export, through the ports, of old and useless horses and of thoroughbreds" (Lewis,1980a). Horses were too valuable for working purposes to be exported, unless their working days were completely over.

In 1943, "Owing to the increased tillage operations and further deterioration in the transport position, it was found necessary to retain in the country any horses which could be utilized as workers or vanners, and licences have only been issued for the export of old and useless horses, unfit for working purposes, and of thoroughbreds"(AGR,1943-4).In the same year, in the Republic, the registration of Irish Draught sires reached a peak, even though the total number of Clydesdales and Shires was three below the peak of 81 that they had reached in 1940. During the 1939-43 period, and for a further three years, working horses played an essential, almost dominant, role in maintaining the economy of the Republic of Ireland.

By 1st December, 1944, conditions had eased sufficiently in the Republic "...to relax the restrictions so as to permit the export of geldings of all types." The flood gates had opened and the demise of the horse as a work animal in Ireland was at hand, even though that might not have been immediately apparent, for "The total number of horses in the country [RI] in June, 1945, was 464,520, an increase of 5,654 on the preceding year" (AGR,1944-5).

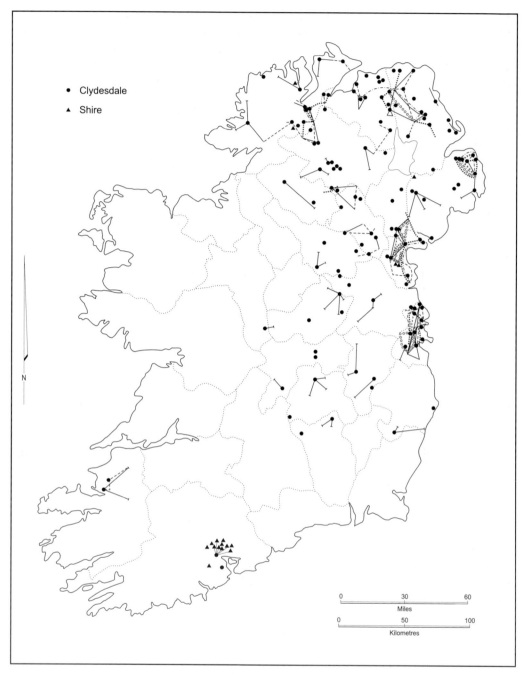

Figure Eleven: *Clydesdale and Shire stallions registered under the Horse Breeding Scheme of the Department of Agriculture in 1921. Partly because of Departmental restrictions, Clydesdales were largely restricted to the Province of Ulster and to Counties Louth and Dublin. Shires concentrated just north of Cork city, to provide heavy draught horses for the city hauliers. Since Clydesdales, in particular, travelled extensively for their mares, it is difficult to depict the intertwining networks of some regions. Similar networks still existed in 1939, as the Registers of Stallions for that year show, but farm mechanization following the end of the Second World War rapidly ended the travelling stallions system for these heavy draught horses. (Redrawn from Lewis, 1980a)*

Post-war exports

In 1945, following the end of the Second World War, exports of horses were allowed subject to quotas on the numbers that could be sent to various states. 300 horses were also shipped to The Netherlands under the Scheme for Relief of Distress in Europe. An important feature of these exports was that they included not only geldings but also mares standing under 15.1 hands in their shoes, the idea being that larger, and supposedly better breeding stock should be retained in Ireland. Significantly, no mares under 15 hands had been registered as Irish Draughts by the inspectors who decided on entrants to the first three volumes of the *Irish Draught Horse Book*.

The beginning of the end

By June 1946 the number of horses in the Republic was just over 12,000 less than it had been a year before. In the same period the number of unbroken horses under one year of age was more than 7,000 less than in the previous year, indicating a general reduction in horse breeding. The number of horses used "...for traffic and manufactures" was 10.3% less than in the previous year and, according to the Annual General Report for the Department of Agriculture for 1946-7, "...trade in horses was generally dull during the year." Heavy draught horses rapidly became a rarity, at least in the Republic of Ireland. The last Shire to be listed in the *Register of Stallions* appeared in 1954, the last Clydesdale in 1967. The situation was not so dramatic in Northern Ireland, where Clydesdales were listed as "...currently earning premiums" in the 1970s, and where some still exist. Nevertheless the number of horses in Northern Ireland declined even during the years of the Second World War so that, twenty years after the outbreak of that War they had reduced by over one third compared with 1939 numbers.

The greatest number of Irish Draught stallions registered for breeding purposes was in 1943, when 197 were listed. Thereafter there was a gradual decline, to 165 in 1950. Numbers decreased rapidly in the years that followed: 125 in 1952, 94 in 1956, but then increased in the economically difficult years of the 1960s to peak at around 110 in 1964. In 1971 there were 119 registered Irish Draught stallions, but only 62 in1978.

Unfortunately, for the years after 1939 there is insufficient evidence to map the distribution and routes followed by Irish Draught stallions in Ireland. In any case, the days of the travelling stallions soon came to an end, and it is doubtful whether any Irish Draughts travelled for their mares after the 1960s. Will Ogilvie has left a wonderful image of travelling stallions in his poem, *The Stallion*. Although Ogilvie probably had heavy draught horses in mind, he captures the splendour, romance and even lust of those former monarchs of the road.

> *Beside the dusty road he steps at ease;*
> *His great head bending to the stallion-bar,*
> *Now lifted, now flung downwards to his knees,*
> *Tossing the forelock from his forehead star;*
> *Champing the while his heavy bit in pride*
> *And flecking foam upon his flank and side....*
>
> *He knows the road and all its hidden fears,*
> *His the staid calm that comes with conquering years....*

He snatches at the clover as he goes,
Clinking the bit-chain as he gathers toll;
He sniffs the speedwell, through wide nostrils blows,
And but for chain and bar would kneel and roll,
His eyes alone reveal in smouldering fire
Pride held in leash, reined Lust and curbed Desire.

For the post 1939 years there is photographic and verbal evidence to suggest that Irish Draughts underwent considerable changes as market forces demanded different sorts of horses at different times. Immediately after the end of the Second World War the demand was for a heavier-type horse suited to an increase in tillage and, when its working days were over, for the booming meat trade. According to Fell (1991) this was met by the selection for registration as Irish Draughts of heavier animals than hitherto: "In selecting these heavier draughts there was an inevitable contamination from the Clydesdale" (Fell,1991). Ultimate responsibility for registering horses as Irish Draughts in the immediate post-war years rested on the Department of Agriculture's inspector, Cooper. He appears to have taken the attitude that a marketable horse was more important than carriage-cum-riding animals, for which there was little trade. Consequently Irish Draughts seem to have become heavier draught animals in the immediate post war years.

Plate Fifty-one: *Charles Sutton competing in the 1940s at a match of the Enniskerry Ploughing Society in Co. Wicklow with his team of heavy Irish Draught type horses. Their white markings suggest an element of Clydesdale breeding, as was typical for that era.* (Photo: courtesy of the late Mr C. Sutton)

By the 1960s it was obvious that there was little future for any horse as a draught animal, and attempts were made to make Irish Draughts more suitable for the riding and sport-horse market. This coincided with the appointment of Sheehy and then R. P. Jennings as the veterinarians who guided the horse breeding programmes of the Department of Agriculture and, later, (in the case of Jennings), Bord na gCapall (The Horse Board), in the Republic. It also coincided with the appointment of a noted horseman as Minister for Agriculture in the Republic, Mr C. J. Haughey.

Mechanisation and slaughter

Throughout the 1960s popular emphasis was placed on mechanisation, as if there was no role for the horse as a working animal. Even the production of pleasure horses seems to have been initially regarded as of little value. Within the Republic there was little attempt even to ensure the registration of more than a few (sixty to one hundred) Thoroughbred sires. An unknown hand has written on the copy of the *Register of Stallions* for 1965 in the library of the Royal Dublin Society, the sad words: "dead", or "sold for slaughter", across the names of many of the draught stallions listed in that document. Seven of the 105 Irish Draught sires were so marked, as was the only Half-bred listed in the Register. The situation was even worse for heavy draught stallions. Of the nine Clydesdales registered, five have their names struck through, two are stated as "dead", two as "sold for slaughter" and one as "exported to N. I.".Within Northern Ireland only three Irish Draught stallions were registered in 1960, plus three Clydesdales, four Thoroughbreds and one "Other". The day of the heavy horse had obviously ended (Lewis,1980a).

The number of horses in Ireland had shown remarkable consistency from 1861 until just before 1951, as Table One shows.

1861	1901	1940	1951	1960	1980
475	435	458	367	223	68

Table One: The horse population of Ireland, 1861-1980 (in 000s)

Between the end of the Second World War and 1951 there was a rapid decrease in the number of working horses and the rate of decrease accelerated during the decade of the 1950s and in the early 1960s. This caused considerable consternation among a number of politically influential horsemen, including C. J. Haughey.

Plate Fifty-two: C. J. Haughey, horseman and politician. As Minister of Agriculture he appointed a Survey Team on the Horse Breeding Industry, which led to the establishment of Bord na gCapall. Haughey subsequently became Taoiseach.

Survey Team on Horse Breeding, 1965

In January 1965, as Minister for Agriculture in the Republic, Haughey appointed a Survey Team on the Horse Breeding Industry. The team reported in August 1966, stating that "...the basis of the Irish half-bred industry is the crossing of Irish Draught mares and thoroughbred sires. With the decline in the number of horses on the land there is a real danger that the foundation stock of Irish Draught mares will disappear...and the bone and substance of the world famous Irish hunter will disappear." The team considered "...that the standard adopted for registration in the Irish Draught Horse Book is not sufficiently high" and recommended publication of a new volume of the Book, listing high quality animals. The report of the Survey team led to a change in Departmental policy on horse breeding and, later, to the establishment of Bord na gCapall (The Horse Board) to cater for the needs of the non-Thoroughbred horse industry.

A national horse breeding scheme, 1968

In 1968 the Department of Agriculture and Fisheries in the Republic "...implemented a national horse-breeding incentive scheme....divided into three sections: mare nominations, foaling premiums, and the provision of suitable stallions"(Yearbook,1975). This led to a marked increase in the number of mare nominations, from 3,242 in 1968 to 9,810 in 1974, although many of the mares were neither Irish Draughts nor Irish Draught in type. There was also a major increase in the number of Thoroughbred stallions registered for service under the scheme, from 97 in 1968 to 232 in 1974, although the number of Irish Draught stallions registered declined from 96 in 1968 to 73 in 1974.

During the 1968-74 period there was an influx of Thoroughbred blood into the Irish Draught herd (O'Toole,2001) This may have been due to an appreciation of market needs by breeders and by R. P. Jennings, the veterinarian overseeing the breeding programmes of the Department who was subsequently the initial Manager of the Breeding Division of Bord na gCapall. The market now required lighter horses than had previously been the case. These could be produced by crossing Thoroughbred sires on Irish Draught type mares, rather than by using heavier, Irish Draught, sires on Irish Draught mares.

Richard (Dick) Jennings, M. R. C. V. S.

Richard (Dick) Jennings was reared on a farm near Skibbereen, in west Cork, and had a great love of horses from an early age: "...as a boy, growing up, I knew the pedigree of every animal at the horse fairs in Skibbereen." After qualifying as a veterinary surgeon in 1948 Jennings initially worked in Professor Martin Byrne's large animal practice in and around Dublin, which handled large numbers of horses. Subsequently Jennings joined the Department of Agriculture as Chief Veterinary Officer. "He was assigned responsibility for the inspection of mares and stallions, and for the purchase of stallions" (Deane,2003). Jennings travelled Ireland up to five times a year, inspecting and registering Irish Draught, Thoroughbred, Half-bred and Pony stallions and mares. "Mares without papers which were good enough, moved well and were good types were given papers. We had to start somewhere."

One of the major problems confronting Jennings was the existence of heavy draught stallions in the Republic, whose influence resulted in the production of "...hairy, inferior mares." "Dick would visit these stallion owners and offer to lease them one of several stallions owned by the Department of Agriculture....Thoroughbred, Irish Draught and Sporthorse [Half-bred] stallions, depending on what the stallion owner

Plate Fifty-three: **Princess Stringy (8865)**, ridden by Brychan Lewis at a
Children's Meet of the Shillelagh Foxhounds, Christmastide 1983. This was
one of the mares without papers that Richard (Dick) Jennings, M. R. C. V. S.,
inspected and that was subsequently registered as an Irish Draught. She later
bred a colt foal to **Positively**, a Thoroughbred stallion that stood with William
(Billy) Barker at Curravanish, Tinahely. (Photo: author)

Plate Fifty-four: **Blue Peter (536)** harnessed to a gig. This 15.3 hands grey
stallion by **Kylemore (459)** out of a mare by **Tipperary Dan (212)**, foaled
in 1959, was inspected and registered by Dick Jennings. Jennings considered
that **Blue Peter (536)** 'was a small horse that had the ability to correct faults
in the mares he covered'. **Blue Peter (536)** was a fruitful sire and, when
standing at the Suma Stud in Co. Meath, fathered **Blue Henry (744)** and
Blue Rajah (759), both of whom had sons on the approved list for the
service of mares in Ireland in 2003. (Photo: courtesy of the Suma Stud)

favoured, were leased at a reasonable fee." Jennings also purchased Thoroughbred stallions for the Department of Agriculture, mainly at the Newmarket and Doncaster sales in England.

"The first thing I looked for [when selecting stallions] was a well-proportioned horse with good quality flat bone, good hocks and free of congenital defects. I had a preference for smaller stallions.... Small horses often have very correct conformation and can improve the progeny of big mares that themselves are not so correct" (quoted in Deane, 2003).Jennings also maintained that "Breeders should not be afraid to use mares of 15.1 hands or 15.2 hands for breeding...in the fall of the year...the foals were often nearly as big as their dams."

Among the Irish Draught stallions that Jennings registered was the 15.3 hands grey, **Blue Peter (536)**, who had many good offspring in the Galway-Mayo region. This stallion traced back in the male line via his sire, **Kylemore (459)**, to **Irish Pearl (193)**, **Pride of Cork (88)**, **Kildare (40)** and **Young J. P. (12)**. All these stallions were grey, 15.3 to 16.1 hands high and came essentially from County Cork, although **Young J. P. (12)** stood with C. Blackmore at Killenaule in County Tipperary when registered (Moore,1993).

Bord na gCapall (The Horse Board)

Bord na gCapall was founded on 8 February 1971. Under the "Bord na gCapall (Assignment of Additional Functions) Order, 1975", the Bord became responsible for administering foaling premiums, mare nominations, the registration of Irish Draught mares, and the purchase and location of Thoroughbred sires for hunter breeding. The Bord also had certain responsibilities for developing markets for non-Thoroughbred horses.

In 1975 the Bord included a list of stallions "...registered with the Department of Agriculture and Fisheries [in 1974] and thus eligible for the service of nominated mares," in its *Yearbook*. From the following year the Bord issued its own publication: *Approved Stallions*. This publication, from 1979 onwards, included stallions standing in Northern Ireland as the Bord and the Department of Agriculture in Northern Ireland co-operated on horse breeding and registration. The 1975 *Yearbook* list stated that "The Register is confined to stallions of the Irish Draught type, to thoroughbreds and half-breds." This suggests that even the Bord was unsure as to whether Irish Draughts were a breed or a type, although the Irish Draught Horse registered numbers were given for all 66 stallions listed as Irish Draughts. The list of Bord na gCapall approved stallions compiled in December 1976 and printed in the 1977 *Yearbook* indicated no such uncertainty: the stallions were shown as Irish Draught.

Irish Draught Horse Society

In 1976 The Irish Draught Horse Society was founded after exploratory meetings had been held at various venues in County Cork. The first exploratory meeting was held at Mary Quinlan's house at Farran, in County Cork. Quinlan had trained as a veterinary surgeon at the Royal Veterinary College in London, but suffered severe injuries in a car crash while a final year student, and could not complete her studies. In 1937 Mary married Maurice Quinlan, who was born in Ballydesmond in County Cork. Initially the couple lived in Sussex, but after Maurice had undertaken war service they bought a small farm at Farran and moved to Ireland.

While in Ireland Mary Quinlan became fascinated by Irish Draughts. Her interest in horses went back to her pre-student days. She had trained her own horse, the son of a Derby winner, and ran him in hurdle races while she was a student.

During the late 1940s and the 1950s Mary Quinlan dealt in horses and ponies, many of which she exported to England. As her business developed so she made contacts with many owners and breeders in Ireland, especially in County Cork. She also became conversant with the pedigrees of many of the horses that she sold and with those of stallions that stood at stud in the County.

The 1970s were a sad period for both heavy and light draught horses in County Cork, as in the rest of Ireland. With increased mechanisation the market for heavy draught animals, which had previously dominated transport in the City of Cork, came to an end. Since 1904 the Department of Agriculture had licensed Shire stallions within a ten miles radius of the City, in order to sire horses for the urban transport market. Light draught horses, which were essentially Irish Draught or Irish Draught type animals, dominated the remainder of the County and were used on the farms and as vanners in the larger towns and in Cork City. They had also been exported in large numbers to Britain and the European continent until they were ousted by the spread of motor vehicles, especially in the 1950s.

By the 1970s motor dealers were importing many second-hand tractors into Ireland, mainly from Britain, and they rapidly replaced the use of horses on the farms. The market for light draught horses in Irish towns had also been ended by increased mechanisation and there was thus little economic reason for farmers to retain their light draught brood mares.

Consequently, in the later 1960s and the early 1970s: "It was a common sight at fairs to see lovely brood mares going for meat, to the distress of the men who were obliged to sell them" (Quinlan,2003).There was thus a great danger that the Irish Draught would soon become extinct. Mary Quinlan decided otherwise and, with the aid of a small but dedicated group of supporters, particularly William Cotter, she inspired people to found the Irish Draught Horse Society. William Cotter was the first Chairman and Mary Quinlan was the first Secretary.

The formation of the Society has been of great importance for the development of the Irish Draught as a breed. In March 1976 Committee members of the new Society met representatives of Bord na gCapall and requested recognition of the Society, subsidies for pure-bred Irish Draught colts, and that Registered Irish Draught mares have their Irish Draught

Plate Fifty-five: *William Cotter, the first Chairman of the Irish Draught Horse Society and a well known breeder of Irish Draughts. (Courtesy of the Irish Draught Horse Yearbook)*

registration numbers shown on their Irish Horse Register passports (Irish Draught Horse Yearbook,1978) The Bord was then in process of establishing a register of all non-Thoroughbred horses in Ireland and of issuing identity documents ("Passports") for all Irish horses and ponies. In 1979, by agreement between Bord na gCapall and the Northern Ireland Ministry of Agriculture, the Irish Horse Register was extended to include animals in Northern Ireland. Documents issued under the Register were officially approved by the International Equestrian Federation (Kennedy,1982).

Breed Standard and Guideline

In 1982 the Irish Draught Horse Society published the *Breed Standard and Guideline* (Irish Draught Horse Yearbook, 1982). The standard states that:

"The Irish Draught Horse is an active, short-shinned powerful horse with substance and quality. Standing over a lot of ground he is proud of bearing, deep of girth, strong of back, loins and quarters. He has exceptionally strong and sound constitution and is known for his intelligence and gentle nature and good sense. Height at 3 years old, stallions 16 hh and over, mares from 15.2 hh with 9 inches or more of clean flat bone."

The standard then stipulates the desired Irish Draught characteristics for head; shoulders, neck and front; back, hindquarters, body and legs; action; and colour. This was the first time that an official standard had been published for Irish Draughts.

1978: The Year of the Breeder

Bord na gCapall designated 1978 as the Year of the Breeder and, through the Mare Replacement Scheme introduced that year, offered "...good breeding mares to approved breeders in certain selected areas who might wish to replace an existing barren or aged mare." Although this scheme was not specifically aimed at Irish Draught mares, it was of value to the breed, as was the Mare Purchase Scheme. Under the latter scheme "Persons interested in acquiring a non-thoroughbred brood mare for the first time will be eligible for a grant of £100 providing the mare is suitable and approved by the Bord." Both these schemes were introduced "...on a pilot basis" in Donegal/Leitrim, North West Mayo, Kerry, Clare, Roscommon and Galway (excluding Connemara).

In 1979 Bord na gCapall collected details of all mares that visited stallions under the breeding schemes of 1978 in the Republic and in Northern Ireland. 1,269 registered Irish Draught mares visited stallions. These mares came from three main regions: east Galway-Clare-north Tipperary, west Cork, and the Ballina area of Sligo. Hardly any Irish Draught mares from Northen Ireland went to a stallion (Lewis,1981).

The Non-Thoroughbred Horse Industry Study, 1979

In December 1979 a study of the non-Thoroughbred industry was published that had been commissioned by Bord na gCapall and carried out by An Foras Taluntais (the Agricultural Institute). This study included geographical information proving that in 1975, expressed in terms of numbers per 1,000 acres of crops and pasture, non-Thoroughbred horses were most common east of a line from Drogheda to Cork, with secondary concentrations in Clare, west Cork, Limerick and east Galway. These (with the exception of County Dublin, which was a heavy draught horse area), were essentially the regions in which Irish Draught stallions had been most common in 1939, the last year for which information on stallions that travelled for their mares is available. The study also showed an increase in the number of non-working and non-Thoroughbred horses during the 1970s and concluded that "The size of the non-thoroughbred herd is increasing at a satisfactory rate." Less satisfactory, however, was the discovery that Irish Draught mares, on average, were four or five years older than Half-bred mares (O'Neill *et al.*,1979).

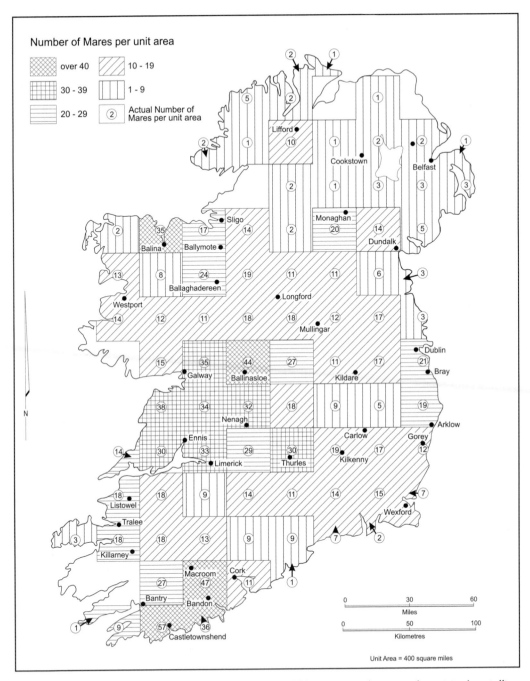

Figure Twelve: *Registered Irish Draught mares per 400 square mile areas that visited a stallion under the horse breeding scheme of 1978. The greatest number of mares was in Clare and adjacent areas of Galway and Tipperary, as well as in west Cork.* (Redrawn after Lewis,1983)

Pedigrees

The late 1970s and the 1980s were years in which increasing interest was focussed on the pedigrees of Irish Draughts. In 1978 Bord na gCapall, which was by then the body responsible for registering horses as Irish Draughts, and for maintaining the records, decided to close the *Irish Draught Horse Book* to all but the progeny of registered parents. According to Cotter (2003) the Bord "...reserved the right to introduce Thoroughbred blood from time to time" (Cotter,2003). As Lewis (1982) wrote: "Effectively, therefore, the Irish Draught is at last being transformed from a type into a breed."

In 1979 Begg traced the pedigrees of all 64 Irish Draught stallions that were "...currently on the Irish Horse Board Register of Approved Stallions." In a potentially libellous article she claimed that six of those stallions were by a horse that had been sired by a Clydesdale out of a Thoroughbred mare. Her claims do not appear to have been refuted. Begg also drew attention to the four registered Irish Draught stallions that had been sired by Thoroughbreds and the two who had a Thoroughbred grandsire: "...no fewer than a further nine can claim that their dams are by a Thoroughbred." In other words, 21 of the 64 registered Irish Draught stallions were certainly not Irish Draught by pedigree. In fact, Begg wrote that there was only a "...handful of sires descended from old strains of Irish Draught, once regarded as the Irish farmer's workhorse; some say this was the traditional Irish Draught."

Begg concluded that: "The whole idea of fostering the Irish Draught is to retain the inherent genetic factors responsible for abundant resilient bone...a horse that will go on working relentlessly day after day, and show no signs of wear either in his temperament or physical make-up; a stamp of horse whose size and appearance is easily recognised as Irish Draught. It is these genes that the breeder should be trying to preserve within his Irish stock." She also noted that: "If Irish Draughts are to be regarded as a breed, then under E. E. C. legislation the Stud Book would have to be closed in the near future to all except the progeny of animals already recorded on the existing Register, i. e. of traditional Irish Draught bloodlines, providing they measure up to minimum standards (height and bone measurement)."

Three years later, in 1982, Lewis discussed breeding and the Irish Draught and regretted that "...few breeders know much about the lineage of individual Irish Draughts", which he blamed on the fact that few volumes of the *Irish Draught Horse Book* had been published. He pointed out that, by using the manuscript records lodged in the Bord na gCapall archives, it was possible "...to trace the pedigrees of many sires." Lewis added that:

"...just because a horse traces back in direct male descent to one of the Irish Draught foundation sires, does not necessarily mean that the horse is a true-blue Irish Draught. **King of Diamonds [547]**, for instance, is out of a mare believed to have been sired by the Half-bred, **True Boy**. Admittedly, **True Boy** had a line back to **Kildare (40)**, but he was nevertheless not wholly Irish Draught."

Lewis concluded that "...given the present state of the Irish Draught "breed", direct male descent is probably the best indication that one is breeding a 'genuine' Irish Draught."

Inspections and the resurgence of the Irish Draught

The published report of the Bord na gCapall team who inspected horses in1982 encouragingly stated that there was "...discernible improvement in Irish Draught youngstock." They expressed the opinion that credit was due to breeders "...and to the tireless workers from Bord na gCapall, particularly the breeding manager Dermot Forde." They noted that "There are still far too many unsuitable animals" brought for inspection and that "The types and variations of animals brought out for registration throughout the country are sometimes remarkable."

The inspectors concluded that "...it must not be forgotten that Bord na gCapall has played an important role in the campaign to save the Irish Draught and the resurgence of the breed and its newly re-emerging quality has been in no small part due to the efforts of the officials and the volunteers [who helped in assessing animals submitted for registration] who have given unsparingly of their services over the past few years" (Irish Draught Horse Yearbook, 1982). Perhaps the self-praise was a reaction to the controversy that in 1982 surrounded Bord na gCapall and its registration of stallions. In 1987 the Bord was disbanded and, two years later, officially dissolved.

Society registers Irish Draughts

Responsibility for inspecting and registering horses as Irish Draughts was handed over by the Bord to the Irish Draught Horse Society in 1983. The Northern Ireland branch of the Society had already been formed in 1978 and the first Irish Draught mare inspections in Northern Ireland had been held in 1980. A sister society, the Irish Draught Horse Society of Great Britain, had been founded in 1979 and already organised its own breeding incentive schemes. In 1988 the Northern Ireland branch of the Irish Draught Horse Society inaugurated its own foal incentive scheme.

Appendix Irish Draught scheme

In 1982 an Appendix Irish Draught scheme was introduced in order to increase the very low number of registered Irish Draught mares and to improve the quality of the Irish Draught Horse population. In 1986, for example, there were only 748 live Registered and Appendix Irish Draught mares, but numbers increased to a peak of 1,755 in 1993 (O'Hare,2002a). Mares of suitable type, with at least three registered Irish Draught grandparents and no foreign blood, were eligible for registration as Appendix Irish Draught mares as long as they passed inspection. The last Appendix Irish Draught mares were registered in 1992 and just over 1,260 mares were registered under the scheme. Filly foals by registered Irish Draught stallions out of Appendix Irish Draught mares were eligible for full Irish Draught registration. Between 1990 and 1997, 337 mares registered as Irish Draughts were out of Appendix mares, accounting for almost 37% of all Irish Draught mares registered in those years (O'Toole,2001).

Irish Draught Horse Incentive Scheme, 1990-1994

The disbanding of Bord na gCapall in 1987 was followed in November 1989 by the nomination, by the Minister for Agriculture in the Republic, of a fourteen member Horse Advisory Committee (Willis,1992).This was followed in1990 by the initiation of the Irish Draught Horse Incentive Scheme, which operated from 1990 to 1994. Under this scheme a grant of £400 was offered for every live pure-bred foal by a registered Irish Draught stallion out of an Appendix or fully registered Irish Draught mare. This scheme proved beneficial in that the percentage of Irish Draught and Appendix mares covered by registered Irish Draught stallions rose from 44% in 1988 (before the scheme was introduced) to 65% during the time covered by the scheme. Once the scheme ended the percentage fell again to approximately 43% (O'Toole,2001)

Quality Mare Retention Scheme, 1994-1999

In 1994 the Irish Horse Board Co-operative Society Limited (which is the successor of Bord na gCapall and was founded in 1993 as a joint venture between the Minister for Agriculture and the breeders), initiated a scheme to support non-Thoroughbred horse breeding. The scheme was part funded by the European Union's Operational Programme for Agriculture, Rural Development and Forestry (Irish Horse Register,1995). Mares, selected on the basis of conformation, soundness and performance, qualified for two payments of £500 each for two foals sired by Approved stallions. A total of £1.5 million was allocated to the scheme, which operated until 1999, but only two-thirds of the money was utilised. The rest had to be returned (O'Hare,2002c). 1,172 mares qualified for the scheme, of which 327 were descended from **King of Diamonds (547)**, whose breeding is discussed in Chapter Seven. Not all of these mares were Irish Draughts. Although the scheme was of value to Irish Draught breeders it was not aimed specifically at them and its effect on the breed is difficult to evaluate.

The Garda Mounted Unit (Police horses)

In 1998, after urging by members of the Irish Draught Horse Society, An Garda Síochàna (The Irish Police) formed a Mounted Unit, with stables at Áras An Uachtaráin (the Presidential Lodge) in Dublin. The Unit uses geldings at least 16.3 hands high, preferably dark bay or grey. Irish Draught geldings are considered ideal for the Unit. Although it is unlikely that The Garda Mounted Unit will ever employ more than a handful of Irish Draught geldings, it is hoped that the Unit will attract other police customers for the breed. The Californian Mounted Unit, for example, has almost 500 horses; the London Metropolitan Police have over 150; New York has over 160. There is thus a potential market for large Irish Draught geldings in police work overseas as well as in their home country.

Dangerously low numbers: an endangered breed

During the 1990s there was a decrease in the percentage of foals sired by Irish Draught stallions and entered in the Irish Horse Register, from 38% in 1990 to 21% in 1999. During the same period there was an increase in popularity as sires of what are now called Irish Sport Horses. These are Half-breds with varying amounts of Thoroughbred and Irish Draught in their pedigrees.

O'Toole wrote in 2001 that "The Irish Draught Horse is numerically a small breed." She then stated that "There are approximately 900 mares and 90 stallions in the current population." The market for Irish Draughts has declined almost continuously since the end of the Second World War so that, no matter how important they are as foundation stock for hunter and Irish Sport Horse breeding, few breeders can afford the luxury of producing them. In 1999 only 45% of registered Irish Draught and Appendix mares were covered by registered Irish Draught stallions.

According to the Food and Agriculture Organisation of the United Nations, a population with less than 1,000 females and 20 males is endangered. The American Livestock Breeds Conservancy considers any breed with less than 1,000 annual registrations to be endangered. The Irish Draught Horse is thus, at the beginning of the twenty-first century, one of the world's endangered breeds.

Plate Fifty-six: *Irish Draught geldings are excellent for police work. Those used in the Mounted Unit of An Garda Síochàna, like this horse, are at least 16.3 hands high.* (Source: *Solid Silver*)

Chapter Seven

AN ENDANGERED BREED: WHAT OF THE FUTURE?

The brood mare herd in the new millennium

In 2001 the Breeding Committee of the Irish Draught Horse Society undertook a survey of the brood mare herd, which consisted of Appendix and registered Irish Draughts. The Committee was concerned at the decline in the number of mares at stud, the proportion being bred pure, and the low registration rate. The Committee considered that the breeding herd was in a similar position to that of the mid 1980s and noted that herd size had decreased from 1,755 in 1993. In 2000 only 727 Registered and Appendix Irish Draught mares produced foals, and only 271 of the foals were by an Irish Draught sire (O'Hare,2002a).

In order to increase the size of the herd the Irish Draught Horse Society met the Irish Horse Board Co-operative Society in 2001. The meeting agreed that the Appendix Register should be reopened. Applicant mares should have one registered Irish Draught parent and three registered Irish Draught grandparents. An Amnesty Registration scheme was also agreed, whereby mares whose pedigrees were verified as full Irish Draught for two generations could be registered. "The society observed that there were mares in the national herd which were Irish Draught but which could not be registered because their dams had not been registered." The Society also suggested "...that older mares could be registered free of charge provided they met the normal registration criteria" (O'Hare,2002a).

The reopening of the Appendix Register and the Amnesty scheme were, of course, desperate measures, justified only by the extremely low number of registered Irish Draught mares. The number of mares inspected and accepted for full registration as Irish Draughts in 2000 was only 165, yet that was the highest number for over a decade. 83.6% of mares inspected were accepted for registration in that year. By offering registration and breeding schemes approved by the Irish Horse Board it was possible for Irish Draught breeders to tap into European Community funds, especially the Structural Funds and the International Fund for Ireland.

European Community regulations

In 1993 the horse industry in Ireland became subject to the European Communities (Equine Stud-Book and Competition) Regulations. Under these regulations horses were supposed to be registered in officially recognised stud books. In 1992 the European Commission had already stipulated that each member state must have a national authority to which organisations maintaining or establishing stud books in that state must apply for recognition. The Department of Agriculture became the national authority in Ireland.

In order to comply with European Community regulations the Irish Horse Board was delegated responsibility for operating the Irish Sport Horse Stud Book. This Book is an outgrowth of the Irish Horse Register that was established in 1974 by Bord na gCapall. "Studbook regulations provide for stallion inspection, performance testing and classification, mare and progeny registration with lifetime documentation backed by bloodtyping and DNA verification when required" (O'Hare,2002b).

The Irish Sport Horse Studbook

Under the Draft Rules and Procedures of 5 October 1994 relating to the Irish Horse Register, it was stated that five "corebreeds" were eligible for classification as stallions in Ireland: Irish Draught, Irish Sport Horse, Irish Riding Pony, Connemara Pony and Thoroughbred. In addition, stallions of the following breeds could also be classified: "Hannoverian, Full Arab, Anglo-Arab, Trakehner, Westfalea, Holsteiner, Dutch Warmblood, Belgium Warmblood, Selle Francais [sic], Weatherby's Non-Thoroughbred which have established studbook pedigree, and other breeds which may be added from time to time" (Irish Horse Register, 1995). Stallions of heavy draught breeds are excluded from the Irish Sport Horse Stud Book.

Under European legislation all horses in Europe must be eligible for registration in some studbook. Stallions are registered under three categories: Approved, Supplementary 1 (S1) and Supplementary 2 (S2). For a stallion to be Approved he must be inspected for conformation and undergo a veterinary examination for soundness, and must participate and qualify in performance testing. The only exceptions are racehorses that have proved themselves on the track.

In 1998 the Irish Horse Board introduced performance testing for all categories of stallions, apart from some racehorses (O'Hare,2002b). Stallions of established pedigree that pass conformation and veterinary examinations and obtain sufficient points in performance testing, are registered as Approved Stallions. Stallions which are sound and have established pedigree, but which fail to pass all the criteria for Approved status, are registered as S1. There are two S2 categories. The first is for sound stallions which do not have established pedigrees, the other is for stallions which fail the veterinary examination and do not have established pedigrees but which have "...high performance in competition, provided he is of a suitable breed type."

Performance testing

Performance testing for stallions was introduced in 1991 and "... was organised by the Breed Societies in conjunction with the Department of Agriculture, Food and Forestry". "The scheme received financial assistance from the Operational Programme for Rural Development", in other words, it was partly funded by the European Union (Irish Horse Register, 1995).

Bord na gCapall had already emphasised the importance of performance by sending one of its Irish Draught stallions, **Flagmount Boy (683)**, showjumping in 1979. At that time Nicholas O'Hare, the well-known Irish equestrian writer and commentator, opined that "Irish Draughts are not really competition horses in the modern showjumping sense, and [**Flagmount Boy**] is not a horse of international calibre." O'Hare continued: "Of the 178 pure bred Irish Draught foals born last year...78 were colts and 100 were fillies. The fillies have ...an obvious and vital part to play in developing new infra structure for Irish breeding, but the role of the colts is not so clear....what are breeders to do with young horses which are really too heavy to become competition horses in the accepted sense, and are not acceptable as stallions....How many Irish Draught stallions do we require?"

Plate Fifty-seven: *John Hall on **Flagmount Boy (683)**, a 16.3 hands grey horse sired by **King of Diamonds (547)** out of **Gowran Betty (7561)**, bred by Martin Brophy of Flagmount, Clifden, Co. Kilkenny. The horse was purchased by Bord na gCapall in 1976. After being broken and jumped in competitions at the Kellet Riding School, this stallion was leased to John McCarthy of Drimoleague and covered mares successfully in west Cork between 1977-79. **Flagmount Boy (683)** was then returned to show jumping, reaching what was then Grade C, but died before he could be sent back to stud. (Courtesy of the Irish Draught Horse Yearbook)*

As the market for horses in the last decade of the twentieth century focussed increasingly on athletic animals suited for competitive equestrian sports, so performance testing of potential sires became extremely important. Under testing introduced by the Irish Horse Board, stallions were required to complete a small show-jumping course. Alternatively, they could attend "...a system of central performance testing...for a period of several days" (O'Hare,2002b).In the new millennium Irish Draught and Sport Horse stallions are expected to loose jump or be ridden over a course of jumps, and then be examined for conformation, movement and satisfactory temperament. Those that satisfy the examiners are Approved, while others may be classified as Supplementary. The latter may be required to undergo either testing in competitive show jumping (where they have to gain a minimum of 30 points under Show Jumping Association of Ireland rules) or participate in and satisfactorily complete a ten to twelve week testing by the Horse Board before being Approved. Those that fail either test remain on the Supplementary Register.

Although the cost of performance testing is appreciable, and the Irish Draught Horse Society's Breeding Committee requested in 2000 that it should be dropped, it is important for the marketability of all Irish horses that such testing should continue. In addition to performance testing, stallions are also evaluated on conformation, athleticism and temperament. The scoring system for these attributes, as used in 2002, was: type and presence 20; pedigree 20; conformation: head 5, neck 5, shoulders and withers 20, body 20, topline 20, hindquarters 20, forelimbs and feet 25, hind limbs and hocks 25; movement: forelimbs 25, hind limbs 25; athleticism 50; temperament 20. Over 50% is required before a stallion is Approved.

In spite of the cost and reasonably rigorous nature of performance and conformation testing, the number of Irish Draught stallions has increased over the twenty year period from 1983 to 2002 inclusive, from 72 to 95 Approved stallions plus 72 Supplementary Book stallions. Whether these are too many Irish Draught stallions for the small number of mares in Ireland, of all breeds, is debatable. O'Hare (2002c) has even suggested that the proliferation of stallions may terminate "...the time honoured country stallion tradition, with the commercial yards of the twentieth century [where mares were brought to be served by stallions that covered many mares] going the way of the travelling stallion procedures which prevailed in the nineteenth."

Sport horse or farm horse?

During the 1970s the support of Bord na gCapall for the Irish Draught as the foundation stock for the breeding of non-Thoroughbred Irish horses led to the revival of the breed, as did the formation of a breed society and the holding of classes for Irish Draughts at the Dublin Horse Show and at many other venues. By the 1990s, however, some commentators condemned the horses as being "...an agriculturally based type which has little to offer modern breeding" (O'Hare,2002b). Irish Draughts, it was said, were too slow and heavy to be fully competitive in equestrian sports, while the days of the work horse were over. What, then, of the future?

O'Toole (2001) had already shown that the input of Thoroughbred blood in the Irish Draught had increased in the short period from 1977 to 1980, when the amount of Thoroughbred genes reached 13% in the reference population that she studied. Sires such as **Clover Hill (665)**, and **King of Diamonds (547)**, both of which have had tremendous influence on the breeding of Irish Draughts in the last two decades of the twentieth century, carried Thoroughbred blood close up in their ancestry. Both horses sired many winners on the show jumping circuit, and their progeny (and many of their descendants) are highly marketable. **King of Diamonds (547),** according to returns to the World Breeding Federation over six years ending in 1996, was the seventh leading sire in the world on progeny achievement (O'Hare, 2002c). Neither horse, by any stroke of the imagination, could be considered the typical light draught farm animal of the

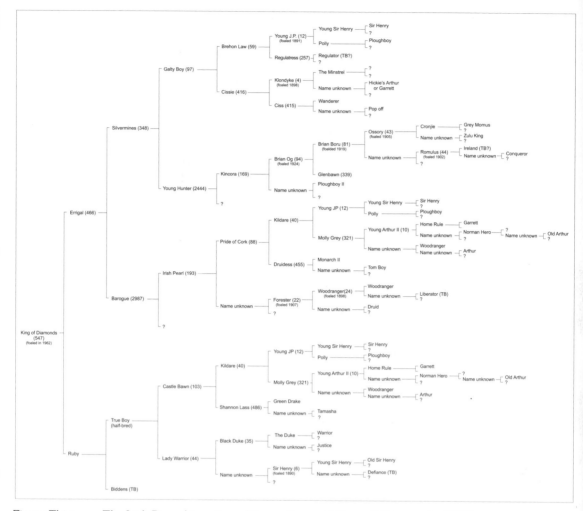

Figure Thirteen: *The Irish Draught portion of the pedigree of **King of Diamonds (547)***

Second World War and subsequent horse-meat trade years, although both might well have held their own in the carriage trade of earlier times.

King of Diamonds (547) was sired by **Errigal (466)** out of **Ruby**, who was by the Half-bred stallion **True Boy**. The **King** was foaled in 1962 and was a chestnut horse bred by the O'Neills of the Slyguff Stud, Bagenalstown, County Carlow. **Ruby** was out of the Thoroughbred mare, **Biddens**. Apart from this Thoroughbred the **King's** breeding was genuine Irish Draught, going back to **Young J. P. (12)** on the direct male line and via **True Boy**, who was by **Castlebawn (103)** out of the Irish Draught mare **Lady Warrior (44)**. Perhaps **True Boy** should have been registered as an Irish Draught! His male line traces back to **Kildare (40)** and hence to **Young J. P. (12)**.

King of Diamonds (547) was campaigned on the show jumping circuit when produced by John and Mary Hutchinson of Kilkenny, and became a Grade A show jumper, he was thus thoroughly performance tested. The **King** then stood with Thomas and Loftus O'Neill at Slyguff Stud where he was a most successful stallion in the 1970s and 1980s. When the **King** died, in 1991 at the age of 29, he had thirty four descendant stallions in the

Plate Fifty-eight: *Loftus O'Neill with* **King of Diamonds (547)**. (Photo: courtesy of Maymes Ansell)

Irish Draught portion of the stallion register and was the premier sire of show jumpers in Ireland.

Clover Hill (665) was foaled in 1973 and was a brown horse of 17 hands, by **Golden Beaker**, who was a Thoroughbred by **Arctic Storm**. The dam of **Clover Hill (665)** was an unregistered mare named **Ohilly Beauty**, and she was by the grey Irish Draught, **Tara (369)**. The sire of **Tara** was the chestnut stallion **Forest Hero (298)**, foaled in 1936 and got by Florence Crowley's 15.2 hand grey horse foaled in 1920: **Clonmult (91)**. **Clonmult (91)** was by the famous16.1 hands grey sire that had stood with Mrs Fitzgerald at Clonmult: **Kildare (40)**. The dam of **Clonmult (91)** was an unregistered mare by **Young Arthur II (10),** the 16.1 hand grey stallion foaled in 1895 who was, in turn, sired by the unregistered **Home Rule** by the famous hunter getter: **Garrett**. The dam of **Tara (369)** was the Irish Draught mare **Union Hall (1697)**, by the 16.1 hand grey **Woodranger (24)**, foaled in 1898 and by the unregistered sire of the same name. **Woodranger (24)** was out of a mare by **Liberator**, which according to O'Hare (2002a) was a Thoroughbred.

Close inspection of the pedigree of **Clover Hill (665)** shows that he descends from **Garrett** via lines through **Kildare (40)** and the unregistered mare from which that famous sire got **Clonmult (91)**. There is thus considerable similarity and shared breeding in **Clover Hill (665)** and **King of Diamonds (547)**, emphasising the narrow genetic base from which modern Irish Draughts have developed.

Unlike **King of Diamonds (547)**, who was tested and proven in the showjumping arenas of Ireland, **Clover Hill (665)** never underwent any sort of performance testing, except that of his virility as a stallion. The lack of performance testing probably does not matter, since recent work by Aldridge (2000) has shown that the breeding value of sires for the production of show jumpers can be evaluated through the performances of their progeny, even if the sires themselves were never competitively tested.

Clover Hill (665) was bred in County Galway by Stan Page. When he was two years old he was noted as a potential stallion by Dick Jennings, the veterinarian who

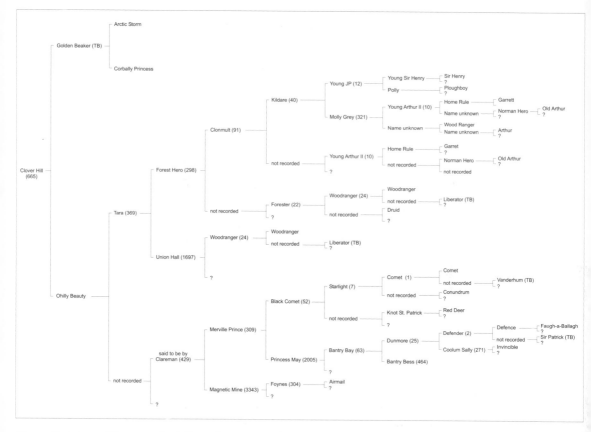

Figure Fourteen: *The main Irish Draught portion of the pedigree of* **Clover Hill (665)**. **Airmail (215)** *was a great grandson of* **Prince Henry (5)**, *as shown in Figure Twenty-one.*

oversaw the Department of Agriculture's and subsequently Bord na gCapall's horse breeding programmes. By the 1970s Jennings had realised the need for producing lighter and more athletic Irish Draughts than in the days of the true draught animal. Jennings also apparently realised the role that Thoroughbreds have played in the production of Irish Draughts, and he was not afraid to select stallions for registration as Irish Draughts even if they had Thoroughbred blood close-up in their pedigrees, as long as they had suitable Irish Draught characteristics.

      Clover Hill (665) began his stud career in 1976 and stood for the rest of his life with Philip Heenan in County Tipperary, at the Ringroe Stud, Borrisokane. The horse died in 1997, by which time he had sired 1,730 registered foals. Breeders soon realised that the progeny of **Clover Hill (665)** were good jumpers and, by the time he died, the stallion had assumed the mantle formerly held by **King of Diamonds (547)** and was the leading Irish sire of show jumpers. O'Hare (2002a) even suggests that **Clover Hill (665)** might be the more outstanding sire, although "This...has yet to be proved." Presumably O'Hare was unaware, when he wrote, of the meticulous genetic evaluation of show jumping horses and their sires by Aldridge (2000). Through her research Aldridge proved, statistically, that **Clover Hill (665)** was a slightly better sire of show jumpers than **King of Diamonds (547)**.

O'Hare quotes a letter of Tony Power's, the Irish racing correspondent, in which Power wrote:

> "It is no surprise that Clover Hill was a success. His sire Golden Beaker and Golden Beaker's dam Corbally Princess were both tough old battlers that won their share of races and Golden Beaker kept winning over three seasons as a sound, honest horse....Clover Hill's sire line produced courageous, sound horses; horses that could race and could be taught to jump."

Clover Hill (665) ranked 12th in the World Breeding Federation for Sport Horses listing of leading sires of show jumpers over the period 1991-2001. During the same period **King of Diamonds (547)** slipped to 21st place. Through her analysis of show jumping performances by sires and their progeny over the period 1993-1999 Aldridge (2000) showed that **Clover Hill (665)**was the second highest ranking Irish Draught sire for the production of show jumpers over that period, while **King of Diamonds (547)** ranked fifth, below his son: **Diamond Lad (695)**, **Sea Crest (728)** and the leading sire of all breeds, the Irish Draught son of **Clover Hill (665)**, **Coille Mor Hill (840)**.

The descendants of **Clover Hill (665)** at the start of the new millennium included both **Coille Mor Hill (840)** and **Mackney Clover (867)**. The former stallion had 30 Grand Prix wins to his credit by 2001 and already, at the 2000 registration, had 135 foals registered. O'Hare (2002a) considers that **Coille Mor Hill (665)** "...is the breed's flagship at the start of the twenty first century. Without him the Irish Draught would have very little impact on the jumping scene." More important, O'Hare notes the Thoroughbred blood in the recent pedigree of **Coille Mor Hill (665)** and argues that "Thoroughbred blood has brought performance to the Irish Draught...if the breed is to blossom as a performance breed in the years ahead, special attention will have to be given to those bloodlines which carry Thoroughbred and...perhaps, more importantly to bring in outside blood once more."

Genetic analyses

Although Thoroughbred blood is a well known ingredient in the pedigrees of Irish Draughts, O'Toole (2001) has drawn attention to the contribution of other blood lines in the composition of the breed. She has written that "A population can be characterised genetically [by looking] at the genealogical structure of the breed." Furthermore, analyses of pedigree records makes it possible to assess the risk of losing genetic variability. "In small populations there is a risk of losing genetic variation due to the small number of breeding animals."

The reference population

O'Toole (2001) studied all 1,319 Irish Draughts for which there are records in Ireland and Britain and that were born from1997 to 2000 inclusive. She argued that "...they represent the future breeding stock of the Irish Draught population." 43% of this reference population was male and 57% female. She found that "Thoroughbred genes account for just over 8% of the genes in Irish Draught horses born between 1997 and 2000", although between 1977 and 1980, when breeders and Bord na gCapall were trying to produce more athletic animals, the figure reached 13%. Since the *Irish Draught Horse Book* was closed in 1979 (except for a few qualified admissions), the percentage of Thoroughbred genes has been in decline.

Inbreeding

When O'Toole examined the extent of inbreeding among the Irish Draught population that she studied she found that the coefficient of inbreeding was generally very low, and not cause for genetic concern. "Inbreeding", she wrote, "is the mating together of individuals that are related to each other by ancestry." She also wrote that "...it is desirable to keep inbreeding at a low level in horse populations."

Geneticists measure the extent of inbreeding by examining pedigree data and expressing it in terms of a formula that was devised by Wright in 1923.This formula shows the inbreeding of an animal as a percentage, which is called the *coefficient of inbreeding*. In their natural environments horses have low coefficients of inbreeding. Too much inbreeding usually leads to loss of vigour, loss of stamina, decrease in fertility and an increase in hereditary diseases. Mammals experience appreciable reduction in vitality and in reproduction when the coefficient reaches, or exceeds, 10%.

O'Toole found that horses in her reference population (those foaled from 1997-2000 inclusive) have an average inbreeding coefficient of only 0.86%. This is far less than the coefficients for many other breeds. Table Two shows the coefficients of inbreeding calculated for different breeds using pedigree data extending over five generations.

Arab	Trotter Français	Anglo-Arab	Thoroughbred	Irish Draught	Selle Français
3.08	1.86	1.17	1.02	0.86	0.7

Table Two: Coefficients of inbreeding for different breeds of horses
(Note: the coefficients are expressed as percentages based on five generation pedigree data analyses. Source: O'Toole, 2001.)

O'Toole concluded that the low coefficient of inbreeding for Irish Draughts indicated that "...the mating of related individuals was deliberately avoided." On the basis of the low coefficient there is no obvious cause for concern about the genetic viability of Irish Draughts now or in the near future.

The influence of founder animals

Geneticists commonly study the influence of *founder animals*. These are *either* the first born animal listed in a pedigree, for which no parents are known; *or* if only one parent of an animal is known, that parent is regarded as the founder animal. The influence of founder animals is shown as the percentage of genes in the sampled population that trace back to that animal. When O'Toole studied her reference population she found that the most influential animal among her Irish Draughts was **Ruby**, the dam of **King of Diamonds (547)**. This mare, as already discussed, was out of a Thoroughbred by an Irish Draught sire that traced back to **Young J. P. (12)**. She also traced back, via the dam of her sire, to another foundation sire: **Sir Henry (6)**. **Ruby** contributed 3.55 % of the genes of the reference population, whereas the next most influential animal, the mare **Grey Glen (10403),** contributed 2.6%. Most other founder animals contributed under 1%. There is thus no major cause for genetic concern on the basis of the undue influence of any founder animals. **Grey Glen (10403)**, incidentally, goes back to **Comet (1)** if her ancestry is traced back, as well as to **Young J. P. (12)**.

Plate Fifty-nine: **Clareman (429)**, a chestnut horse by **Merville Prince (309)** out of **Magnetic Mine (3343)** and born in 1948, was descended in the male line from **Comet (1)**. **Comet (1)** was foaled in 1892 and was a brown horse of 16.2 hands that belonged to James Doran of Enniscorthy. Although **Clareman (429)** stood with D. MacNamara near Tuamgraney in Co. Clare, he later stood with Mrs Margaret O'Toole at Carnew in Co. Wicklow, not far from Enniscorthy. (Photo: Bord na gCapall archives)

Foundation stock

Breeders use the term *foundation stock* to refer to animals that they consider to be very important in the development of a breed. Unfortunately, however, it is not always easy to quantify the influence or importance of foundation stock as opposed to other animals that have contributed to a pedigree. The foundation stock for Irish Draughts are commonly considered to be the stallions **Young J. P. (12)**, **Prince Henry (5)**, **Comet (1)**, **Young Arthur (9)**, and to a lesser extent **Sir Henry (6)**, **Young Arthur II (10)**, **Black Duke (35)** and **Woodranger (24)**. Some of these horses have descended only through female lines and are thus not as well known as those whose influence can be traced through direct male descent.

Ancestor contributions

Rather than consider *foundation stock*, geneticists study *ancestor contributions*. In other words, they calculate the percentage of genes in a given population that can be traced back to one ancestor. O'Toole (2001) discovered that the most important ancestor in her reference population was **King of Diamonds (547)**, who contributed just over 7% of the genes in the population. The stallions that came next in importance were **Ben Purple (580)** and **Milestone (498)** with contributions of a little more than 5% each.

Glenside (563) was in fourth position with 3.6% and the noted jumping sire, **Clover Hill (617)** was next with rather more than 3%. Nearly 50% of the genes of the reference population came from only seventeen ancestors. These facts suggest that there is a real risk that in the near future the Irish Draught population may be over dominated by certain ancestors, and that the "…genetic diversity [of the breed] could decline."

O'Toole also discovered that 10% of the stallions produced 50% of the breeding female offspring and 30% of the breeding male offspring in her reference population. These facts bode ill for the future of the breed, since they mean that a few stallions are dominant, to the detriment of genetic conservation.

The generation interval

The generation interval in breeding is the average age of parents when their offspring are born. From the genetic viewpoint this is an indication of the rate of genetic throughput in a population. O'Toole found that in 1980 the generation interval was 10.7 years. By 2000 it had grown to 12.2 years. In other words, on average stallions and mares were starting to breed later in 2000 than they did twenty years earlier. This means that the movement of genes through the population is slower than formerly, although this may not necessarily be genetically detrimental to the population.

Breed composition

O'Toole also looked at the breed composition of Irish Draughts. In other words, she assessed the contribution of genes from different breeds that existed in her reference population (which was essentially the population of Irish Draughts at the start of the new millennium). She discovered from analyses of pedigrees that 55.5% was Irish Draught, 8.7% Thoroughbred, 5.5% Irish Sport Horse (this category would formerly probably have been called Half-bred), 0.5% Appendix Irish Draught, 30.3% "Other".

The Irish Draught, in spite of being essentially a closed Stud Book horse, is by no means a pure breed, it contains a very large percentage of genes from other breeds. O'Toole commented that the modern market requires horses that are athletic, that are suitable for equestrian sports and especially showjumping. "…a more athletic type Irish Draught may require more thoroughbred in its breeding, which may improve performance, but would tend to reduce or eliminate whatever Irish Draught genes [are] still in the population."

Lewis (1981) had already shown, based on a four generation study of pedigrees, that there were important spatial differences in the breed composition of Irish Draught mares. In an area of east Cork-west Waterford in 1978, for example, just over 29% of the ancestry of registered Irish Draught mares was Thoroughbred. In Cavan Thoroughbreds contributed 17% of the ancestry while in the Gorey area of County Wexford the Thoroughbred input was only 5.5%. Further research into such spatial distribution patterns may be valuable for identifying areas in which the Irish Draught population is more "pure" than elsewhere.

Demographics

When O'Toole looked at the demographics of her reference population she came up with the astounding discovery that, as the breed entered the new millennium, "…each Irish Draught mare does not even produce one pure bred filly foal as a replacement in her lifetime." If this trend continues the Irish Draught is doomed to extinction and the breed, if that is what it is, will no longer exist.

Conclusions

After all her meticulous research O'Toole concluded that "...if this unique genetic resource is to continue its role in present day breeding then it will have to be carefully managed as a rare genetic resource to ensure its long term survival."

Whither now for the endangered breed?

O'Hare (2002b) was forthright in his comments on the genetic findings. To manage the breed as a rare genetic resource would necessitate "...an input of funding from the state and commitment and expertise from breeders." He was of the opinion that the future of the breed lies in the sporting performance of Irish Draughts: "Without it, the Irish Draught filly will go nowhere as a suitable brood mare for the general horse breeder." In O'Hare's opinion the future of the Irish Draught is as a riding horse, and this means that the Irish Draught must become an increasingly athletic and lighter animal. In order to achieve this aim there will, he thought, have to be a greater infusion of Thoroughbred blood. "The breed is changing. Horse breeding in the twenty first century is about evolution. The Irish Draught must change...."

Ever since hot-blooded sires were crossed on the Hobbies that had developed in Ireland by the sixteenth century, and the Irish warm-blood began to evolve, evolution has been the name of the game.

The Irish Draught, as described to the Commissioners on horse breeding in 1896-7 was probably a somewhat different animal from the presumably warm-blooded carriage horses that had pulled Lady Ossory's carriage into Dublin in 1670. The rearing leader that was one of the team pulling a carriage past Frascati in 1781 was obviously warm-blooded! The horses that pulled Bianconi's passenger vehicles in the first part of the nineteenth century were probably finer and faster horses than the Irish Draughts that worked on the land at the end of that century, but they probably shared many common blood-lines, even if documentary evidence for that is lacking. The Irish Draughts that were first registered under that name in the early years of the twentieth century differed in many ways from the meatier animals of the post-Second World War meat trade days.

There is little historical reason to object to additions of Thoroughbred blood in order to lighten the breed and make Irish Draughts more marketable, although care must be taken that there is not too much loss of bone. Whether infusions of European warm-blood genes are desirable, or whether they will destroy the conformation and character of the Irish Draught, is as yet unknown. Nevertheless there are a number of European warm-blood stallions in Ireland in the new millennium and they will undoubtedly influence the future of horse breeding in the country.

Understanding the genetics of the Irish Draught depends partly on analyses of pedigrees and these, for breeders and owners, are of the utmost importance. The final chapter is therefore devoted to the pedigrees of the main Irish Draught families and to the new bloodlines that are now influencing the breed.

Chapter Eight

PEDIGREES

Initial records

The first stallions to be registered as Irish Draughts by the Department of Agriculture, and to have their pedigrees recorded, were born in the 1890s. **Comet (1)** was foaled in 1892 and was a brown horse of 16.2 hands belonging to James Doran of Enniscorthy in County Wexford. He was by the unregistered **Comet** out of a mare by the Thoroughbred **Vanderhum** who, as stated in Chapter Six, was first included in the RDS *Register of Thoroughbred Stallions* in 1892, when he belonged to Kevin Mullins of Glenmore in Co. Kilkenny. **Defender (2)** was a 16.1 hands grey belonging to John O'Donohoe of Tullow in County Carlow, although this stallion was born in 1900. **Hibernia (3)** was a 16 hands bay stallion foaled in 1895 and the property of Andrew L'Estrange of Mullingar in County Westmeath. **Klondyke (4)**, foaled in 1898, was a 16.1 hands grey belonging to John O'Neill of Labasheeda in County Clare. **Prince Henry (5)** was a 16.1 hands grey foaled in 1894, by the unregistered **King Henry** out of a mare by the equally unregistered **Eclipse**. He belonged to Richard G. Cleary of Streamstown in County Westmeath, and so the list continues.

Of the first ten stallions listed in the *Irish Draught Horse Book*, **Sir Henry (6)** had the distinction of being the oldest, having been foaled in 1890. He was a 16.1 hands grey belonging to Denis Treacy of Thomastown in County Kilkenny.

In some cases the sires and grandsires of the stallions were also recorded, as were the sires of the dams. The pedigrees of certain Irish Draughts can thus be traced back to the last decades of the nineteenth century, although few details other than the names are now known of the unregistered ancestors of the breed. Nevertheless it is apparent that the first registered Irish Draughts contained infusions of Thoroughbred blood, from horses such as **Vanderhum** and **Liberator**.

Major sire lines, 1979

The first major analysis of the pedigrees of Irish Draughts that was published and freely available was that of Begg (1979) She traced the ancestry, in the male line, of all Irish Draught stallions approved for the service of mares in Ireland in 1979. Begg discovered that the stallions mainly traced to four sires registered in the first volume of the *Irish Draught Horse Book*. These were **Comet (1)**, **Prince Henry (5)**, **Young Arthur (9)** and **Young J. P. (12),** each of which founded a family. Another family that had a major impact on the breeding of Irish Draughts was that of **Woodranger (24)**, a grey horse standing 16.1 hands, foaled in 1898 and that came from Durrus in County Cork, where he belonged to Henry Love. Unfortunately the direct male line of this family ended in the 1960s. The bay horse **Ferrybridge (623)**, foaled in 1966 and the property of Dan Horgan of Lisselton in County Kerry, was the last born colt of the family to be registered as a stallion. Begg also found that a new family had been introduced in the 1940s, based on **Laughton (446)**. Additionally, some Irish Draught stallions were sired by Thoroughbreds.

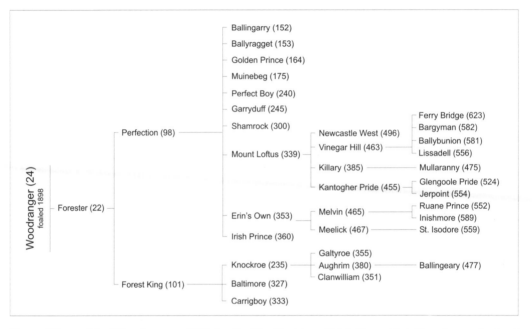

Figure Fifteen: *The **Woodranger (24)** family. The Registered Irish Draught stallion descendants of the grey 16.1 hands **Woodranger (24)**, foaled in 1898 and by the unregistered **Woodranger** out of a mare by **Liberator,** are shown from left to right. The direct male line died out with the **Ferrybridge (623)** generation.*

During her researches Begg discovered that there was considerable chicanery relating to pedigrees, if what her informants told her was correct. Some breeders, or sellers, apparently told prospective buyers the pedigrees they thought the buyers wished to hear, rather than the truth! In one case a stallion registered as an Irish Draught may well have been sired by a Clydesdale. Begg even named the Clydesdale and quoted its registered number. She was also told that the Clydesdale was used on a Thoroughbred mare to produce the offspring that was registered as an Irish Draught with apparently impeccable Irish Draught parentage! Other cases of incorrectly registered parentage were also reported to Begg, but it is impossible to know whether any reliance should be placed on what a minority of her informants told her, they may have been mischievous!

The most numerous Irish Draught family in 1979, in terms of the number of stallions approved for service in Ireland in that year and traced according to their male ancestry, was that of **Young J. P. (12)**, from whom 37 stallions were descended. The other families, in diminishing order of numbers, were those of **Comet (1)**, with 15 approved stallions (six of whom were possibly by a horse of incorrectly stated parentage, and may not have been genuine members of the **Comet (1)** family); **Laughton (446)**, with six representatives; various Thoroughbreds, with five or six offspring depending on whether Begg's informants or the official records were correct; and **Prince Henry (5)** and **Young Arthur (9)** with one stallion each.

Begg noted that the **Young J. P. (12)** family subdivided into two main branches, each of which descended from one of the two sons of **Young J. P. (12)** who have left their mark on the Irish Draught, **Kildare (40)** and **Brehon Law (59)**. In 1979 there were 28 stallions tracing back to **Brehon Law (59)** and nine tracing to **Kildare (40)**.

Major sire lines, 2003

By 2003 there were considerable changes in the sire lines of Irish Draught stallions approved for the service of mares in Ireland, as compared with those of 1979, as Table Three shows.

Family	Comet (1)	Prince Henry (5)	Young Arthur (9)	Young J. P. (12)	Laughton (446)	Clover Hill (665)	Ballynoe Boy (596)	Tb various
1979	15*	1	1	37	6	nil	nil	5 / 6
2003	5**	1	nil	53	9	5	5	

Table Three: *Male line descent of Registered Irish Draught stallions in Ireland, 1979 and 2003*

** Possibly includes 6 by **Abbeylara (476)**
** Possibly includes 2 by **Abbeylara (476)**.
Tb = Thoroughbred. Sources: Begg (1979) and Irish Horse Board web list: www.irishhorseboard.com*

The main changes were that two new sire lines appear to have been introduced, those of **Clover Hill (665)** and **Ballynoe Boy (596)**. **Clover Hill (665)**as stated in Chapter Seven, was sired by the Thoroughbred, **Golden Beaker** by **Arctic Storm**. His dam was sired by **Tara (369)** and thus goes back to **Young J. P. (12)**. Nevertheless, strictly in term of sire line this is a Thoroughbred line, and so is shown as a new male line family. The sire of **Ballynoe Boy (596)** is not known, although his dam was sired by **Clare Man (429)** and thus goes back to **Comet (1)**. **Ballynoe Boy (596)** is thus shown as founder of a new family, although that is, in fact, unlikely.

The Young J. P. (12) family

Analysis of Table Three shows that in 2003 the **Young J. P. (12)**family was by far the most numerous. This family divides into two main groups, that of **Kildare (40)**and that of **Brehon Law (59)**. In 2003 there were seven descendants of **Kildare (40)** in Ireland and 46 of **Brehon Law (59)**. **Young J. P. (12)** had been foaled in 1891 and was a 15.3 hands grey, by the unregistered **Young Sir Henry** out of a dam by the unregistered **Ploughboy**.

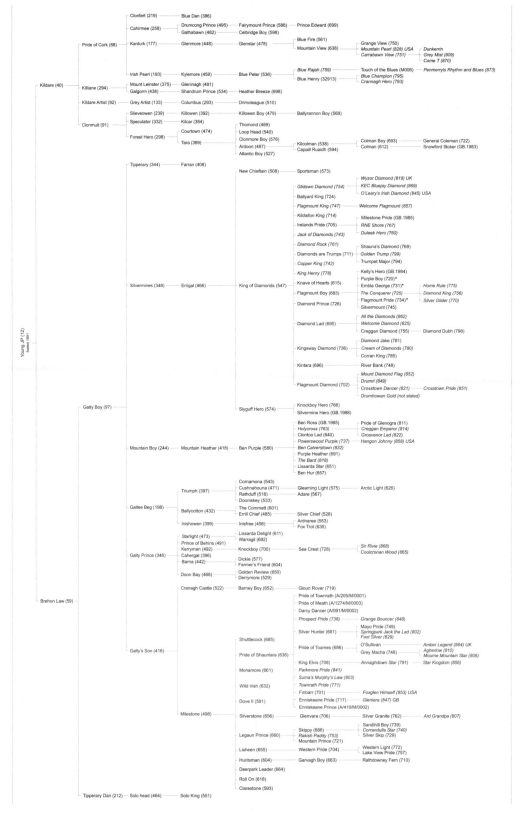

Figure Sixteen: The **Young J. P. (12)** family (abridged, but including the male ancestors of most stallion members of the family foaled in 1970 or thereafter). Stallions whose names are in italics were on the approved list for the service of mares in Ireland in 2003. * Information from Fell (1991)

The Kildare line

The stallions descended from **Kildare (40)**,who was a 16.1 hands grey horse foaled in 1913, were **Blue Champion (795), Blue Rajah (759), Carrabawn View (751), Come T (870), Crannagh Hero (793), Dunkerrin Grey Mist (809), Penmerryls Rhythm and Blues (873)**. Additionally, apparently standing in the United States of America was **Mountain Pearl (828)**.

Kildare (40) sired twenty two Irish Draught sons that were registered for the service of mares. They were **Pride of Cork (88), Garryowen (246), Killane (294), Curragh (143), Kildare Artist (92), O'Donnell Abu (110), Clonmult (91), Kildare Captain (209), Adare (116), Ballyquirke (210), Slievebawn (134), Kildare Guardian (209), Ard Ri (140), Kildare Prince (108), Warrior (102), Kilfera (248), Kildare Duke (117), Silken Thomas (96), Irish Champion (87), Irish Rebel (188), Killester (118)** and **Castlebawn (103)**. At the start of the new millennium it was the family sired by his son, **Pride of Cork (88)** that was important as a stallion getting line.

Pride of Cork (88) had at least ten Irish Draught registered stallion sons, two of whom, **Irish Pearl (193)** and **Kanturk (177)** founded families that continue into the twenty-first century. The **Irish Pearl (193)** family descended via **Kylemore (459)** to the sire that Dick Jennings registered when he saw him in County Galway, **Blue Peter (536)**. This horse, when standing at the Suma Stud in County Meath, was a fruitful sire and his two sons, **Blue Henry (744)** and **Blue Rajah (759)** had descendant sons on the list approved for the service of mares in 2003.

Kanturk (177) was represented at the beginning of the new millennium by **Carrabawn View (751), Come T (870)** and **Dunkerrin Grey Mist (809),** with **Mountain Pearl (828)** in the USA.

The Brehon Law line

Brehon Law (59) was a 16 hands grey horse, foaled in 1916, that sired only two Irish Draught sons that were registered for the service of mares. One of them, **Galty Boy (97)**, sired nine registered stallion sons, four of whom sired lines that still exist in male descent: **Silvermines (348), Mountain Boy (244), Galty Prince (346)** and **Galty's Son (416)**.

Brehon Law's (59) descendants in the new millennium are: **Agherlow (810), All the Diamonds (862), Annaghdown Star (791), Ard Grandpa (807), Ben Calverstown (832), Coolcronan Wood (865), Copper King (742), Corrandulla Star (740), Cream of Diamonds (780), Creggan Emperor (814), Crosstown Dancer (821), Crosstown Pride (851), Diamond King (756), Diamond Rock (761), Drumri (849), Drumhowan Gold (not stated), Duleek Hero (760), Fast Silver (829), Flagmount King (747), Glidawn Diamond (754), Golden Trump (799), Grange Bouncer (848), Grosvenor Lad (822), Holycross (763), Home Rule (775), Jack of Diamonds (743), KEC Bluejay Diamond (869), Kildalton King (714), King Henry (778), Mount Diamond Flag (852), Mourne Mountain Star (806), Parkmore Pride (841), Powerswood Purple (737), Prospect Pride (738), Rakish Paddy (753), RNE Shore (767), Silver Glider (770), Sir Rivie (868), Springpark Jack the Lad (802), Star Kingdom (856), Suma's Murphy's Law (803), The Bard (818), The Conqueror (725), Townrath Pride (771), Welcome Diamond (825), Welcome Flagmount (857)**. Additionally, **Amber Legend (864)** stood in England, while

Foxglen Himself (853), **Glenlara (GB) (847)**, **Hangon Johnny (858)** and **O'Learys Irish Diamond (845)** stood in the United States of America.

Galty Boy and Tipperary Dan

Of the two stallion sons of **Brehon Law (59)**, **Tipperary Dan (212)** was important as a sire of brood mares, particularly the dam of **Blue Peter (536)**, who was the ancestor of Irish Draught stallions registered for the service of mares in Ireland in 2003. His other son, **Galty Boy (97)**, a grey horse of 16 hands foaled in 1922, sired nine stallions: **Galtee Beg (198)**, **Black Prince (242)**, **Mountain Boy (244)**, **Galty Rover (302)**, **Tipperary (344)**, **Galty Prince (346)**, **Silvermines (348)**, **Galty's Son (416)** and **Newbridge Boy (460)**.

Silvermines (348) has been of great importance as the ancestor of the showjumping family of **King of Diamonds (547)**;while **Galty's Son (416)** sired **Milestone (498)** and thus gave rise to the **Pride of Shaunlara (636)** family as well as the

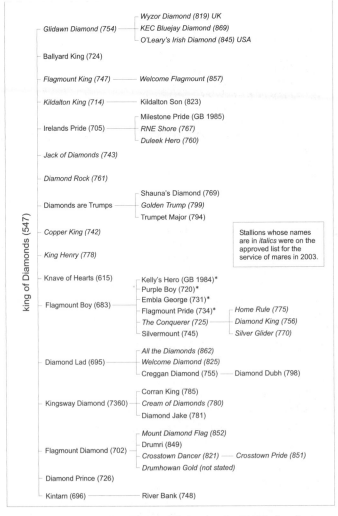

Figure Seventeen: *The **King of Diamonds (547)** family.*
* Information from Fell (1991)

less numerically important families of **Legaun Prince (660)** and **Silverstone (656)**. **Mountain Boy (244)**, another son of **Galty Boy (97)**, gave rise to the family represented in the new millennium by **Holy Cross (763)** and his sons, as well as other stallions.

King of Diamonds

King of Diamonds (547), whose pedigree was discussed in Chapter Seven, has had a tremendous influence on the recent development of the Irish Draught (O'Hare,2002c), with at least seventeen Irish Draught stallion sons, eight of whom had Irish Draught stallion sons approved for the service of mares in Ireland in 2003. Some of these stallions have impressive showjumping records, as have many of their progeny, and they are probably the most important Irish Draught family, economically and possibly genetically (as O'Toole's (2001) research suggests), at the start of the new millennium. Nevertheless they are strongly challenged and may be eclipsed by the **Clover Hill (665)** family, if Aldridge's (2002) statistical evaluation of breeding values for the production of show jumpers is an accurate predictor of the future.

Plate Sixty: ***Pride of Shaunlara (636)***, *a 16.2 hands grey stallion by* **Milestone (498)** *out of* **Boston Burglar (6440)** *by the Thoroughbred* **Prefairy**, *foaled in 1969 and bred by John Hoolan. After moving to Marily Power's and Susan Lannigan O'Keefe's Suma Stud in Co. Meath the* **Pride of Shaunlara (636)** *was schooled and ridden and sired many offspring. (Photo: courtesy of the Suma Stud)*

Pride of Shaunlara

    Pride of Shaunlara (636) was bred by John Hoolan, foaled in 1969 and grew into a 16.2 hands grey horse of immense presence. He was sired by **Milestone (498)** and was out of a mare by the Thoroughbred horse **Prefairy**. **Pride of Shaunlara (636)** sired at least fourteen Irish Draught registered sons who were approved for the service of mares. Of these, **Pride of Toames (686)**, **Silver Hunter (681)** and **King Elvis (708)** were numerically very important as the sires of approved stallions by 2003. Two sons, **Finbarr (701)** and **Enniskeane Pride (717)** sired sons that, in 2003, stood in the USA, **Foxglen Himself (853)** and **Glenlara (847)**.

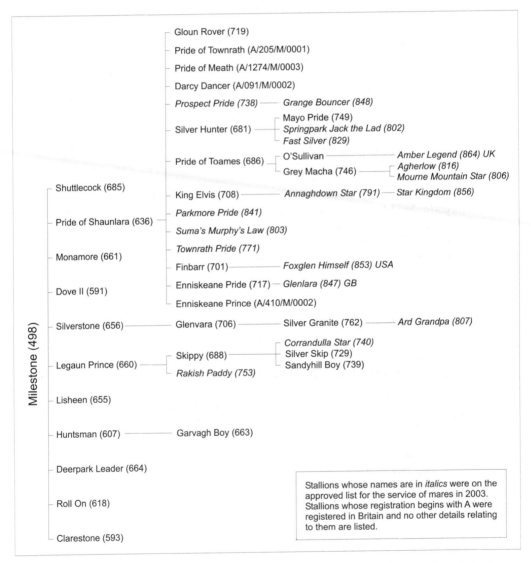

Figure Eighteen: *The **Milestone (498)** family, which includes **Pride of Shaunlara (636)***

Plate Sixty-one: *The 16.1 hands grey stallion,* **Pride of Toames (686)**, *sired by* **Pride of Shaunlara (636)** *and foaled in 1975, combined the families of* **Young J. P. (12)** *through his sire's male line and of* **Comet (1)** *via* **Glen Lad (458)**, *the sire of his dam* **(Toames Beauty 7260)**. *Two of his sons* **(O'Sullivan** *and* **Grey Macha;746)** *sired three colts that were approved for the service of mares in Ireland in 2003* **(Amber Legend (864)UK, Agherlow (816), Mourne Mountain Star (806))**. **Pride of Toames (686)** *was bred by John McSweeney of Toames West, Macroom, Co. Cork. (Courtesy of the Irish Draught Horse Yearbook)*

The Comet (1) family

In 2003 there were only five Irish Draught stallions approved for the service of mares in Ireland and standing in that country that traced back in the male line to **Comet (1)**. These were: **Donovan (859), It's the Quiet Man (830)** and **Golden Warrior (752)**, plus two stallions tracing back via **Abbeylara (476)**, whose parentage was questioned by Begg (1979): **Brown Lad Lara (758)** and **Clonakilty Hero (860)**. Additionally, in the USA stood **Ri an Domhan (813)**, who traced back via **Golden Warrior (752)**.

Comet (1) had eight sons who were registered as stallions: **Blazing Star (53), Shelldrake (72), Jupiter (54), Satellite (30), Starlight (7), Meteor (29), Sunbeam (55)** and **Zeppelin (15)**. Only two of them sired major dynasties: **Sunbeam (55)** and **Starlight (7)**. Of these, **Starlight (7)** is normally considered the more important in that he has direct male descendants.

Sunbeam

Sunbeam (55), who was a 16.2 hand black horse foaled in 1914, was bred by John Lee but belonged to Robert Casey of Dingle in County Kerry when registered. He sired **Bright Ray (144)**, a 16.1 hand bay owned by John McNamara of Tuamgraney of County Clare. This horse sired fourteen stallions: **Ormond (338), Dalcassian (222), Clontarf**

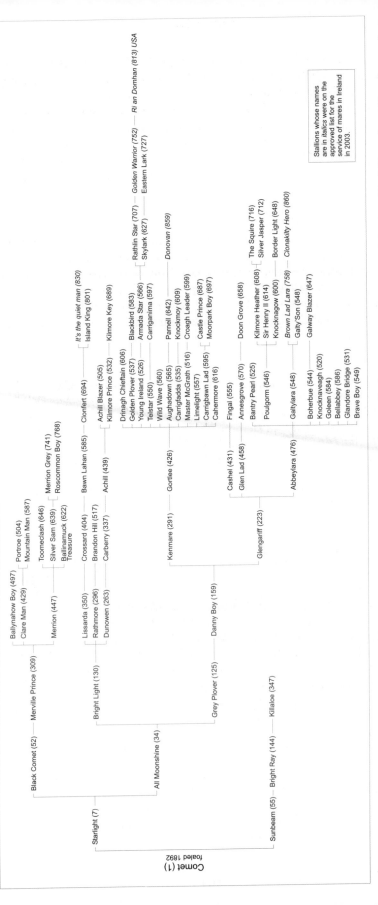

Figure Nineteen: The **Comet (1)** family as it existed in male descent in the late twentieth and early twenty first centuries. Registered Irish Draught stallion descendants of **Comet (1)** are shown, by generation, from left to right. The **Sunbeam (55)** family only exists in brood mares and is therefore shown in abridged form.

(171), Mountshannon (174), Ardnacrushna (199), Corofin (205), Lough Derg (221), Eagle's Nest (254), Slieve Bernagh (261), Torpedo (299), Bright Boy (303), Sun Ray (306), Avondale (421) and the grey: **Killaloe (347)**, foaled in 1941 and registered with J. L. O'Toole of Carnew in County Wicklow. **Killaloe (347)** sired the dams of two registered Irish Draught stallions, **Courtown (474)** and **New Chieftain (508)**, which were registered in Counties Limerick and Kerry respectively when they belonged to John Ryan of Cappamore and James Healy of Ardfert. Some of **Sunbeam's (55)** other sons also sired stallion descendants, but **Sunbeam's (55)** line now exists in brood mares.

Starlight and the All Moonshine line

Starlight (7) sired eight registered Irish Draught stallion sons: **Drumbeg (38), Lucky Star (50), Black Comet (52), Rainbow (49), All Moonshine (34), Southern Cross (69), Bright Star (58)** and **Pride of Breffnin (46)**. **All Moonshine (34)** and **Black Comet (52)** have proved the most important. **All Moonshine (34)** was a15.3 hand bay horse that was foaled in 1913 and was registered as the property of Denis Reardon of Dunmanway in County Cork. He sired four registered stallions, of whom **Bright Light (130)** and **Grey Plover (125)** have proved of continuing value to the breed.

Plate Sixty-two: *The 16.15 hands grey stallion,* **Clonfert (694)**, *was foaled in 1976 and went back in the direct male line to* **Comet (1)**. *Through the sire of his dam this stallion traced back to* **Prince Henry (5)**. *His son,* **It's the quiet man (830)**, *stood at stud in Ireland in 2003, even though* **Clonfert (694)** *had been exported to England where, by 1980, he stood at stud with David Cosby at Holsworthy in Devon.* **Clonfert (694)** *also participated in the parade of Hunters Improvement Society stallions before Her Majesty the Queen at Peterborough. (Photo: courtesy of Kit Houghton)*

Bright Light

Bright Light (130) was a 16.1 horse who proved himself by fathering eight registered Irish Draught stallions: **Rising Sun (238)**, **Rathmore (296)**, **Dunowen (263)**, **Brightnet (216)**, **Knocknagow (272)**, **Rising Light (288)**, **Duhallow (203)** and **Lissarda(350)**. The latter was the grandsire of the influential and "very strong...old fashioned Draught" **Bawnlahan (585)**(McMahon in Fell,1991). **Bawnlahan (585)** was the grey sire of the equally grey 16.1 hands **Clonfert (694)** who stood in Leitrim before being exported to England where he stood with David Cosby. **Clonfert (694)** had magnificent bone and was well suited to produce heavy weight hunters. An Irish Draught son of **Clonfert (694)**, the 16.3 hands grey **It's the Quiet Man (830)**, was an approved stallion in Ireland in 2003.

Grey Plover

Grey Plover (125) was a 16 hands grey who sired **Danny Boy (159)**, from whom descended the roan **Kenmare (291)** and the 15.2 hands chestnut **Glengariff (223)**, who was supposedly the sire of the 17 hands chestnut **Abbeylara (476)**. Begg (1979) maintained that **Abbeylara (476)** was actually by a bay Clydesdale named **Rocavan Reformer (24677)** out of a Thoroughbred mare.

Donovan (GB) (859) and **Golden Warrior (752)**, both approved for the service of mares in Ireland in 2003, traced back via the **Kenmare (291)** line to **Grey Plover (125)**. **Ri an Domhan (813)**, who was in the USA in 2003, was also of that line. **Donovan (GB) (859)** traced back via **Parnell (642)**, **Aughadown (565)** and **Gortlee (426)**.**Ri an Domhan (813)** and his father, **Golden Warrior (757)**, traced via **Rathlin Star (707)**, **Armada Star (566)**, **Young Ireland (526)** and **Gortlee(426)**.

In 2003 the 16.1 hands brown stallion **Brown Lad Lara (758)** and the 16.3 hands chestnut **Clonakilty Hero (860)** traced to **Grey Plover (125)**, but via **Galtylara (548)**, **Abbeylara (476)**, **Glengarriff (223)** and **Danny Boy (159)**.

Black Comet

Black Comet (52), by **Starlight (7)** by **Comet (1)**, was the grandsire of the grey sire, **Merrion (447)**, who fathered the dam of the 16.1 hand chestnut **Silverstone (656)**. Through **Silverstone (656)** the lines of **Comet (1)** and the **Brehon Law (59)** branch of the **Young J. P. (12)** family were brought together in a horse of magnificent conformation and presence. In the years that followed **Silverstone (656)** sired **Glenvara (706)** the 16.3 hands grey bred by the Honourable Garech Browne.

Through **Merrion (447)**, **Black Comet's (52)** line continued to the 17.2 hands grey **Silver Sam (639)** (who also descended from the **Kildare (40)** branch of the **Young J. P. (12)** family) and thence to the 16.1 hands grey **Roscommon Boy (768)** and the 16.3 hands grey: **Merrion Grey (741)**. The male line then ceased to continue.

Black Comet (52) continued to influence Irish Draughts through the dam's side of a number of Irish Draught stallions approved for the service of mares in 2003.

The Prince Henry family

When Begg analysed the breeding of approved Irish Draught stallions in 1979 she found only one horse that traced directly back through the male line to **Prince Henry (5)**. This was the 16.1 hands chestnut, foaled in 1963, that at some time belonged to D. Healy of Lombardstown in County Cork: **Glenside (563)**. Fortunately, when over twenty

Plate Sixty-three: **Merrion (447)**, by **Merville Prince (309)** out of *Fair Future (3532)* by **Bright Light (130)**, foaled in 1951. **Merville Prince (309)**, a bay horse, was foaled in 1938 and when registered belonged to Jerome Hayes of Drimoleague in Co. Cork. **Merville Prince (309)** was by **Black Comet (52)** by **Starlight (7)** by **Comet (1)**. **Bright Light (130)** was a 16.1 hands bay/dun horse, foaled in 1928 and registered as belonging to Denis O'Reardon of Dunmanway in Co. Cork. He was by **All Moonshine (34)** by **Starlight (7)** by **Comet (1)**. Many Irish Draughts, like **Merrion (447)**, are very closely related, which is probably why they have so many common characteristics. (Photo: Bord na gCapall archives)

years of age, **Glenside (563)** served a mare by **Rusheen Hero (445)** and produced **Glenagyle Rebel (788)**. The great importance of this mating was that **Rusheen Hero (445)** went back in the male line to **Young Arthur (9)**, who was one of the first stallions to be registered in *The Irish Draught Horse Book*. **Young Arthur (9)** was a 16.1 hands grey, foaled in 1898, and by the unregistered **Prince Arthur**.

The **Prince Henry (5)** family became well established through his son, **Irish Guard (13)**. This horse had six stallion sons: **South Mayo (70)**, **Sentry (61)**, **Irish Express (71)**, **Guardsman (56)**, **Dublin Guard (86)** and the great father of stallions: **Irish Mail (60)**. The latter horse sired ten stallion sons, of whom **Carrigeen Lad's (123)** line continues, via **Sunset Lad (419)**, **Glenside (563)** and **Glenagyle Rebel (788)**, in **Huntingfield Rebel (836)**.

Glenagyle Rebel (788), formerly owned by the Suma Stud of Navan, County Meath, sired the only stallion that, in 2003, represented the **Prince Henry (5)** family as an Irish Draught approved for the service of mares in Ireland: **Huntingfield Rebel (836)**. This horse was foaled in 1990 and is just over 16.2 hands high and, like **Prince Henry (5)** and **Young Arthur (9)**, is grey. He covered 45 mares in 2000 and 46 in 2001 and, in those two years, was the sire of 34 colts, although only some of them were pure bred Irish Draughts. The dam of **Huntingfield Rebel (836)** was sired by **Blue Peter (536)**, of the

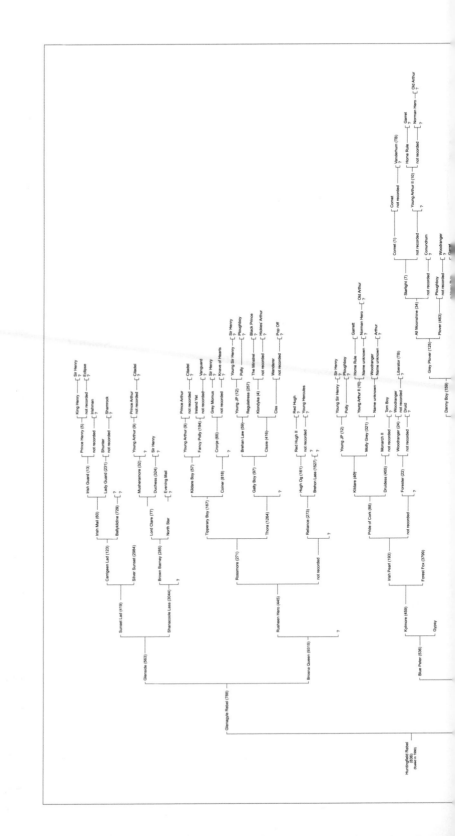

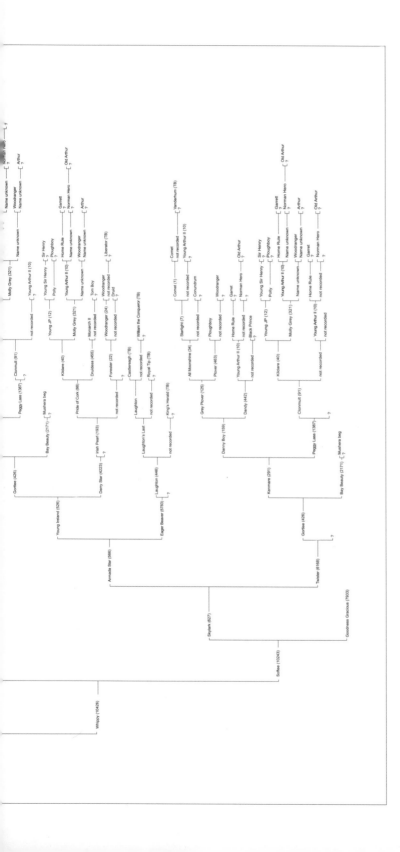

Figure Twenty: *The pedigree of* **Huntingfield Rebel (836)**, *the only Registered Irish Draught stallion to represent the direct male line of* **Prince Henry (5)** *in Ireland at the start of the new millennium.*

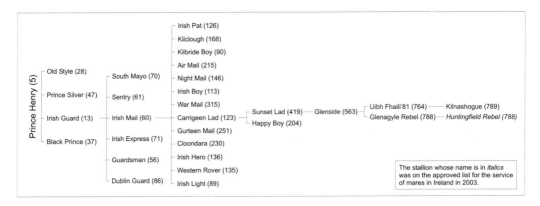

Figure Twenty-one: *The **Prince Henry (5)** family, traced in direct male descent to its sole representative as an Irish Draught stallion registered for the service of mares in Ireland in 2003, showing the registered stallion sons of each main line sire in each generation.*

Plate Sixty-four: **Huntingfield Rebel (836)**, *a 16.2 hands grey horse by **Glenagyle Rebel (788)** out of **Whippy (10426)** by **Blue Peter (536)**, was the only approved Irish Draught stallion in 2003 that traced directly back in the male line to **Prince Henry (5)**. He was foaled in 1990 and bred at the Suma Stud in Co. Meath. In 2001 **Huntingfield Rebel (836)**, ridden by Catriona Stabley, was the Performance Champion at the National Show. Supporters of Irish Draught Horses owe a great debt of gratitude to Susan Lannigan O'Keefe and Marily Power, owners of the Suma Stud, for saving the direct male line of **Prince Henry (5)**. They also, through the dam's breeding of **Huntingfield Rebel (836)**, have retained a line back to **Young Arthur (9)**. (Photo: courtesy of Charlotte Moore)*

Kildare (40) branch of the **Young J. P. (12)** family. **Glenagyle Rebel (788)** was eventually exported to Zimbabwe.

The Young Arthur (9) family

Young Arthur (9), foaled in 1898, was a 16.1 hands grey by the unregistered **Prince Arthur** out of a mare by the unregistered **Citadel**. He was registered as the property of Jeremiah Fogarty of Rathdowney.

Although one stallion in 1979 traced back in the direct male line to **Young Arthur (9)**: the 16 hands chestnut **Rusheen Lad (654)**; none of the stallions approved for the service of mares in Ireland in 2003 did so. **Rusheen Lad (654)** sired **Gortlea Ruler (800),** a brown horse of just over 16 hands that was foaled in 1986 and that subsequently belonged to Mrs Hinckley in Derbyshire in England. Hopefully some of his direct male descendants still exist in that country, if not elsewhere.

Of the Irish Draught stallions approved for the service of mares in Ireland in 2003

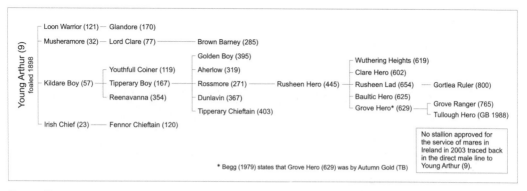

Figure Twenty-two: *The **Young Arthur (9)** family.*

the following trace to the **Young Arthur (9)** male line within three generations back via a female progenitor: **Clonakilty Hero (860)**, out of a mare by **Grove Hero (629)**; **Gold Link (805)**; **Huntingfield Rebel (876)**; **Red Hackle (729)**; **Sammy's Pride (808)**; **Sillot Hill (735)**; **Welcome Diamond (825)**; **Welcome Flagmount (857)**. In the USA, **Hangon Johnny (858)** and in Scotland **Wyzer Diamond (819)** also traced back similarly. The genes of the **Young Arthur (9)** family were therefore still present among the approved stallions of 2003.

Laughton (446) and his family

Laughton (446) was sired by **Laughton's Last**, who won a point-to-point before becoming the favourite hunter of Ikey Bell, a famous Huntsman and Master of Hounds. Bell rode **Laughton's Last** when he was Master of the South and West Wiltshire Foxhounds in England and became famed for his bravery in jumping an iron gate. Apparently it was the horse, and not the rider, who had decided to jump the fearsome obstacle! **Laughton's Last** was by the Half-bred sire, **Laughton**, out of a Half-bred mare by **King's Herald**, a Thoroughbred (Fell,1991). There was thus a great deal of Thoroughbred blood in **Laughton** and therefore in the family that he founded.

The **Laughton (446)** family, judged by the number of stallions approved for service, increased in size between 1979 and 2003. In the latter year there were nine members of the

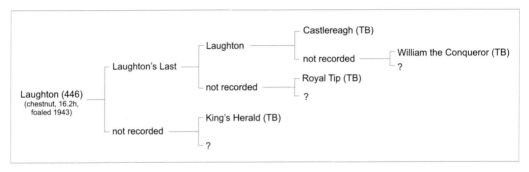

Figure Twenty-three: *The pedigree of* **Laughton (446)**

Plate Sixty-five: **Laughton's Last**, *by Lionel Edwards. Below the painting, and not shown on this reproduction, are the words: To Ikey Bell/ From Lionel Edwards/ 1929* (Reproduced by permission of Mr Hugh W. Newell)

family standing at stud in Ireland and two elsewhere. The nine in Ireland were: **Ballinrobe Boy (703)**, **Castana (837)**, **Classic Vision (827)**, **Corran Ginger (812)**, **Gold Link (805)**, **Naldo (773)**, **Ginger Holly (820)**, **Supreme Ginger (863)** and **Westmeath Lad (834)**. The dam of the last of the above horses was by **King of Diamonds (547)**, although by the end of 2002 the progeny of **Westmeath Lad (834)** had still to distinguish themselves in the showjumping arenas. Two members of the family stood overseas in 2003: **Celtic Gold (838)** in Australia and **Herrero (843)** in the USA.

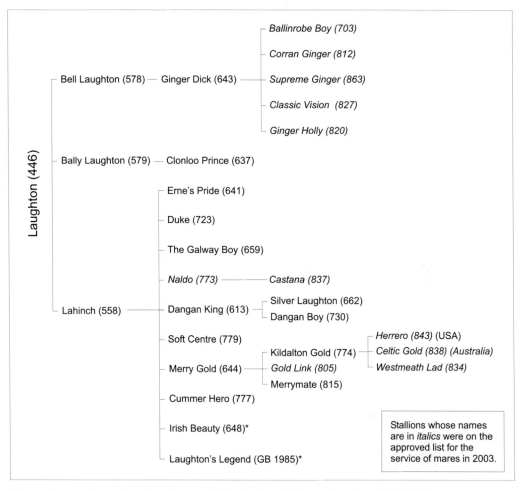

Figure Twenty-four: *The **Laughton (446)** family.* * Information from Fell (1991)

The Clover Hill (665) family

Clover Hill (665) was sired by the Thoroughbred, **Golden Beaker**, so that although his dam was sired by **Tara (369)** and thereby went back to **Young J. P. (12)**, he is classified as the founder of a new family. This family was represented in Ireland by five approved stallions in 2003, three of whom had **King of Diamonds' (547)** blood on their dam's side. They were clearly, therefore, bred with a view to showjumping. These three were: **Diamond Clover (824)**, **Finn's Clover Inn (850)** and **Mackney Clover (867)**. The remaining two members of the family were **Coille Mor Hill (840)** and **Coopers Hill (844)**. Aldridge (2002) has shown statistically, through her genetic evaluation of show jumping horses in Ireland, that **Coille Mor Hill (840)** has the highest breeding value for the production of show jumping animals of all stallions in Ireland, and not just of Irish Draughts.

The Pride of Gloster (847) represented the family in the USA.

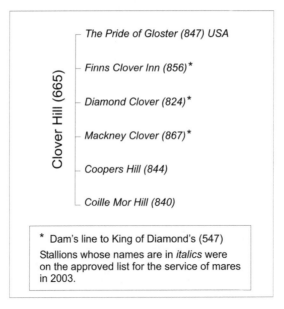

Figure Twenty-five: *The **Clover Hill (665)** family, as approved for the service of mares in Ireland in 2003*

The Ballynoe Boy (596) family

Ballynoe Boy (596) was a chestnut horse of 16.05 hands foaled in 1966. His sire was unknown although his dam was by **Clare Man (429)** and thereby goes back to **Comet (1)**. Technically, therefore, **Ballynoe Boy (596)** is the founder of a new family.

There were five Irish Draught stallions of this "family" approved for the service of mares and standing in Ireland in 2003, all of whom traced back through their dams to

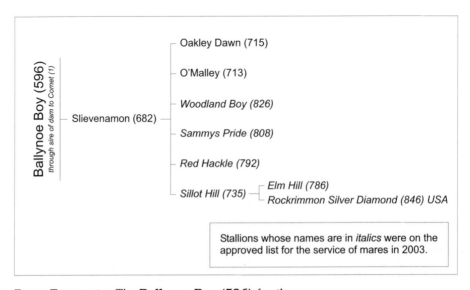

Figure Twenty-six: *The **Ballynoe Boy (596)** family.*

Black Comet (52) and thence to his grandsire: **Comet (1)**. These stallions were: **Elm Hill (786)**, **Red Hackle (792)**, **Sammy's Pride (808)**, **Sillot Hill (735)** and **Woodland Boy (826)**. There was also one member of the family standing in the USA, **Rockrimmon Silver Diamond (846)**, whose dam's grandsire was **King of Diamonds (547)**.

Pedigrees and the future of the Irish Draught horse

Examination of the pedigrees of Irish Draughts, and particularly of the stallions standing at stud in Ireland in the early years of the new millennium, indicates that the Irish Draught Horse is an evolving breed. In the early years of the twentieth century it was essentially a working horse, either on the land or for light draught and riding purposes. In particular, it was suited to military and wheeled transport needs, for which it found a ready market. By 1979, when Begg studied pedigrees, those roles had almost entirely ended and it was obvious that breeders were interested in producing horses that were suited for equestrian sports. This was apparent with the introduction of the **Laughton (446)** line and possibly with the emphasis on some members of the **Brehon Law (59)** line.

By 2003 the emphasis was definitely on the production of show jumpers and other sport horses, and that was evidenced by the introduction of the **Clover Hill (665)** line and the crossing of that line with the showjumping family of **King of Diamonds (547)**. The problem facing those who are genuinely interested in the survival and development of the Irish Draught Horse is how to avoid breeding bone and substance out of the animals and how to retain their calm disposition while, at the same time, rendering them suitable for international competition in equestrian sports. There is a very great danger that, if attempts are made to refine the breed so as to be suitable for speed competitions, as in jump offs in show jumping, the Irish Draught may become just another sport horse and lose the conformation and temperament for which it has been famous for over a century.

The future of Irish Draught Horses is by no means certain. They could be allowed to dwindle into extinction, because production of "traditional" and so-called "pure-bred" Irish Draughts is no longer a paying proposition. Alternatively breeders could change the character of the Irish Draught so that it becomes an increasingly hot-blooded equine, suitable for competitive equestrian sports such as show jumping and eventing at the highest international level. This could be done by increasing the Thoroughbred composition of Irish Draughts, as has been done in the past. Unfortunately that would almost certainly lead to a loss of bone, of stamina, of weight carrying ability and probably of equable temperament. Such losses would be to the detriment of Ireland's reputation as a breeding area for ordinary riding horses as well as for quality weight carrying animals of equable temperament.

There is a final, and preferable alternative. The Irish Draught could be maintained as a rare genetic resource, as an important part of the national heritage of Ireland and as the foundation stock for the production of the Irish Sport Horse: the quality hunters and riding horses and the competitive show jumpers and eventers for which the country is renowned. Care could be given to the preservation of blood lines, such as those of **Prince Henry (5)**, (which has almost vanished in the male line), and **Comet (1)**, which are becoming increasingly rare.

The study of pedigrees has shown that Irish Draughts are dependent for their continuance on suitable, wise and regulated infusions of other blood lines and particularly of Thoroughbred blood. Breeders could, and probably should, be subsidised by the state in order to produce Irish Draughts of suitable character so as to both safeguard the genetic reserves of these horses and to maintain a sufficient foundation stock for the production of more active, and more profitable, Irish Sport Horses. The stud book would have to be opened occasionally so that infusions of Thoroughbred, and possibly other blood, could be made in order to retain the character of the Irish Draught. This might necessitate political action and the modification of existing European Union regulations.

O'Flynn, Chairman of the Irish Horse Board, stated in 2003 that "The Irish Draught horse is our native breed and forms the foundation of our Sport horse industry." Although O'Flynn considered that "...we need more emphasis on 'blood' in our present sports stock," and should therefore "...make more use of the Thoroughbred for our crosses," he believed that "...we must keep the Irish Draught as our foundation" (O'Flynn,2003).

Horses, and especially the Irish Draught horse, are synonymous with Ireland. In 2003 the Minister for Agriculture and Food in the Republic of Ireland wrote that "The Irish Draught gives the Irish Sport Horse its unique characteristic of good temperament, soundness and longevity, and it is essential that an adequate number of Irish Draught mares continue to breed pure....the Irish Draught Horse [is] a very valuable national asset" (Walsh,2003).

"The dainty breed of Hobbies" for which Ireland was renowned in the fifteenth and sixteenth centuries, have gone. In their stead is their successor: the Irish Draught. The cost of subsidising breeders, or even of establishing and maintaining suitable stud farms, would be a small price for Ireland, or even the European Union, to pay for the preservation of the Irish Draught. The Irish Draught Horse is a most important, historic and genetically valuable ingredient of the national heritage of Ireland.

Plate Sixty-six: *A classic Irish Draught mare: Charlotte and Nigel Moore's **Silver Dawn (10231)**, Champion Broodmare at the First National Irish Draught Show, held at the Suma Stud in Co. Meath in 1985. Without quality mares there would be no quality stallions and no quality Irish Sport Horses. Irish Draught mares are, like other Irish Draught horses, part of the national heritage of Ireland.* (Photo: courtesy of Nigel and Charlotte Moore)

REFERENCES

AGR	1903-4 *Annual General Report of the Department of Agriculture and Technical Instruction, Ireland.*
AGR	1904-5 *ibid.*
AGR	1921-2 *ibid.*
AGR	1922-3 *ibid.*
AGR	1943-4 *ibid.*
AGR	1944-5 *ibid.*
AGR	1946-7 *ibid.*
Airy, O.	1886 Butler, James. In: Stephen, L. (editor), *Dictionary of National Biography*, VIII, 52-60.
Aldridge, L. I.	2000 *Genetic evolution of show jumping horses in Ireland.*
Andrews, J. H.	1964 Road planning in Ireland before the railway age, *Irish Geography*, 5, 17-41.
Anon.	2003 The Garda Mounted Unit. In: Deane, E. and Loughnane, A. (editors), Irish Draught Horse Society - 25 Years.
Apperley, N. W.	1926 *A hunting diary.*
Bateman, J.	1883 *The great landowners of Great Britain and Ireland.*
Begg, S.	1979 The Thoroughbred influence and traditional working strains, *Irish Draught Horse Yearbook*, 31-37.
Bence-Jones, M.	1978 *Burke's guide to country houses. Volume I, Ireland.*
Bence-Jones, M.	1987 *Twilight of the Ascendancy.*
Bianconi, M. O'C. and Watson, S. J.	1962 *Bianconi, King of the Irish roads*
Biddell, H. (editor)	1880 *Suffolk Stud Book: Volume One: A history and register of the County Breed of Cart Horses.*
Bowen, M.	1954 *Irish Hunting.*
Burke	1939 *Burke's Peerage.*
Burke	1976 *Burke's Irish family records*
Carden, R.G.	1907 In: de Trafford, Sir Humphrey (editor),*The horses of the British Empire*, 231 ff.
Casserley, H. C.	1974 *Outline of Irish railway history.*
Chivers, K.	1976 *The Shire Horse.*
Clare, E.	1899 Tull, Jethro. In: Lee, S. (editor), *Dictionary of National Biography*, LVII, 304-6.

Cook, W. T. — 1987 The organisation of the Exercise in the Seventeenth Century. In Sanderson, J. (editor), *Change Ringing: the history of an English art*, 68-81.

Cox, M. F. — 1897 *Notes of the history of the Irish horse.*

Cotter, B. — 2003 History of the Society. In: Loughnane, A. and Deane, E. (editors), *Irish Draught Horse Society, 25 Years.*

Cox, M. F. — 1897 *Notes of the history of the Irish horse.*

Craig, M. — 1982 *The architecture of Ireland.*

Crookshank, A and Glin, Knight of, — 1987 *The painters of Ireland c 1660-1920.*

Cullen, L. M. — 1968 *Life in Ireland.*

Deane, E. — 2003 Dick Jennings. In: Loughnane, A. and Deane, E. editors), *Irish Draught Horse Society, 25 Years.*

Delaney, [D.] R. — 1973 *The Grand Canal of Ireland.*

Delaney, V. T. H. and Delaney, D. R. — 1966 *The canals of the south of Ireland.*

Dent, A. — 1978 *Cleveland Bay Horses.*

Dukes, F. E. — 1994 *Campanology in Ireland.*

Ewart, G. E. — 1960 *The horse in the furrow.*

Fairfax-Blakeborough, J. — 1950 *Northern Turf History.*

Fairley, J. S. — 1977 Editor's introduction. In: Stringer, A. *The experienced huntsman*, 3-14. [Original first published in 1714].

Fell, A. — 1991 *The Irish Draught Horse.*

Freeman, T. W. — 1950 *Ireland.*

Garner, W. — 1983 Bindon, Francis. In: de Breffny, B. (editor), *Ireland: a cultural encyclopaedia*, 44.

Gordon, W. J. — 1893 *The Horse World of London.* (Reprinted 1971).

Hall, Mr and Mrs S. C. — 1841-3 *Ireland its scenery, character, etc.*

Heath-Agnew, E. — 1983 *A history of Hereford cattle and their breeders.*

Higgs, H. — 1900 Young, Arthur. In: Lee, S. (editor), *Dictionary of National Biography, LXIII,* 357-363.

Hunter Stud Book VI — 222.

Irish Horse Register — 1995.

Kennedy, M. — 1982 Why the Government thinks a million of its horses. In: Doran-O'Reilly, Q. and Kennedy, M. (editors), *Horses of Ireland,* 201-206.

Lewis, C. A. — 1975 *Hunting in Ireland.*

Lewis, C. A. — 1979 The development and diffusion of the Irish Draught, *Irish Draught Horse Yearbook*, 24-28.

Lewis, C. A. — 1980a *Horse breeding in Ireland and the role of the Royal Dublin Society.*

Lewis, C. A. — 1980b Height characteristics of Irish Draught Horse mares, *Irish Draught Horse Yearbook*, 16-22.

Lewis, C. A. — 1981 Changes in the distribution of registered Irish Draught mares between 1917-19 and 1978, *Irish Draught Horse Yearbook*, 56-61.

Lewis, C. A.	1982 Breeding and the Irish Draught, *Irish Draught Horse yearbook*, 31- 35.
Lewis, C. A.	1983 Irish horse breeding and the Irish Draught Horse, 1917-1978, *Agricultural History Review*, 31, 37-49.
Lewis, C. A. and McCarthy, M. E.	1977 The horse breeding industry in Ireland, *Irish Geography*, 10, 72-89.
Lodge, E.	1827 *Portraits of illustrious personages of Great Britain, vol. I.*
Lodge, E.	1829 *ibid, vol. II*
MacCurtain, M.	1972 *Tudor and Stuart Ireland.*
MacGregor-Morris, P.	1986 *The History of the H.I.S., 1885-1985.*
Mackay-Smith, A.	1978 Foreword. In: Dent, A., *Cleveland Bay Horses.*
Mackay-Smith, A.	1983 *The colonial Quarter Race Horse.*
MacLysaght, E.	1939 *Irish life in the seventeenth century.*
McCracken, E.	1971 *The Irish woods since Tudor times.*
McIlroy, R.	2003 Interview. In: McKenna, M. (editor) *Solid Silver*, 16-18.
Mitchell, [G].F. and Ryan, M.	1998 *Reading the Irish landscape.*
Mitchell, S.	1985 *The dictionary of British equestrian artists.*
Moody, T. W.	1967 Fenianism, home rule and the land war. In: Moody, T. W. and Martin, F. X. (editors), *The course of Irish history*, 275-293.
Moore, C.	1993 *Irish Draught Stallions, 1911-1993.*
Moore, C.	1993 *Irish Draught Mares, 1918-1992.*
Moore, D.	1981 *Foxhounds.*
Mortimer, R., Onslow, R. and Willett, P.	1978 *Biographical encyclopaedia of British flat racing.*
Nolan, W.	1985 Patterns of living in County Tipperary from 1770 to 1850. In: Nolan, W. and McGrath, T. G. (editors), *Tipperary: history and society*, 288-324.
O'Flynn, N.	2003 Ned O'Flynn. In: Deane, E. and Loughnane, A. (editors), *Irish Draught Horse Society, 25 Years.*
Ogilvie, W. H.	1922 The Stallion. In: Ogilvie, W. H., *Galloping Shoes*, 88-89.
O'Hare, N.	1978 Origin of the Irish Draught, *Irish Draught Horse Yearbook*, 6-14.
O'Hare, N.	1979 Ireland's jumping stallion, *Irish Draught Horse Yearbook*, 5-7.
O'Hare, N.	2002a *The Irish Sport Horse.*
O'Hare, N.	2002b *King of Diamonds.*
O'Hare, N.	2002c *The modern Irish Draught.*
O'Neill, F. K., Shanahan, U., Kennedy, M. and McStay, T.	1979 *A study of the non-Thoroughbred horse industry.*
Orme, A.R.	1966 Youghal, County Cork - growth, decay, resurgence. *Irish Geography*, 5, 121 - 149
O'Shea, K.	1914 *Charles Stewart Parnell.*

O'Toole, H.   2001 *Characteristics of the Irish Draught Horse population in Ireland*, unpublished M. Agr. Sc. thesis, National University of Ireland, U. C. Dublin.

Paget, J. O.   1899 Introduction. In: Beckford, P., *Thoughts on hunting* (1899 edition), ix-xxi.

Parker, C. A.   1971 *Mr Stubbs the horse painter.*

Praeger, R. Ll.   1969 *The way that I went.*

Quinlan, J.   2003 Mary Joyce Quinlan, 1912-1994. In: Loughnane, A. and Deane, E. (editors), *Irish Draught Horse Society, 25 Years.*

Stringer, A.   1714 *The experienced huntsman*

Walsh, J.   2003 Foreword. In: Loughnane, A. and Deane, E. (editors), *Irish Draught Horse Society, 25 Years.*

Watson, S. J.   1969 *Between the Flags: a history of Irish steeplechasing.*

Welcome, J.   1982 *Irish horse-racing.*

Whyte, J. H.   1967 The age of Daniel O'Connell. In: Moody, T. W. and Martin, F.X. (editors), *The course of Irish history.*

Willis, G.   1992 *The world of the Irish horse.*

Wright, S.   1923 Coefficients of inbreeding and relationship, *American Naturalist*, 56, 330-338.

Wyndham-Quin, W. H.   1919 *The foxhound in County Limerick.*

Youatt, W.   1843 *The horse.*

BREED STANDARD

Type and character

The Irish Draught Horse is an active short legged powerful horse with substance and quality. Standing over a lot of ground the horse is proud of bearing, deep of girth, strong of back, loin and quarters. Irish Draughts have exceptionally strong and sound constitutions and are known for intelligence, gentle nature and good sense. Height: stallions 15.3 h. h. to 16.3 h. h. approximately. Mares from 15.1 h. h. to 16.1 h. h. Good strong clean bone.

Head

Good bold eyes set well apart, wide forehead and long, well-set ears. Head should be generous and pleasant, not coarse or hatchet headed, though a slight roman nose is permissible. The jaw bones should have enough room to take the gullet and allow ease of breathing.

Shoulders, neck and front

Shoulders should be clean-cut and not loaded. Withers well-defined, not coarse. The neck set in high and carried proudly showing a good length of rein. The chest should not be too broad and beefy. The forearms should be long and muscular, not caught in at the elbows. The knee large and generous, set near the ground. The cannon bone straight and short with plenty of clean flat bone, never back of the knee (calf-kneed) i.e. should not slope forward from knee to fetlock. The bone should never be round or coarse. The legs should be clean and hard with a little silky hair at the back of the fetlock as a necessary protection. In winter the legs may become "woolly" but never should the hair be stiff and coarse or grow down the front of the hoof. The pasterns strong and in proportion, not short and upright nor long and weak. Hooves should be hard and sound, not heavy or contracted, and there should be plenty of room at the heel.

Back, hindquarters, body and legs

The back strong and girth deep with strong loins and quarters, not forgetting the mares must have enough room to carry a foal. The croup to buttocks to be long and sloping, not short and rounded or flat-topped. Hips not wide and plain, thighs strong and powerful and at least as wide from the back view as the hips. The second thighs long and well-developed. The hocks near the ground and generous, points not too close together or wide apart but straight. They should not be out behind the horse but should be in line from the back of the quarters to the heel to the ground. They should not be overbent or in any way weak. The cannon bone short and strong like the front leg or shin and not sloping forward or weak.

Action

Smooth and free but without exaggeration and not heavy or ponderous. Walk and trot straight and true with good flexion of the hocks and freedom of the shoulders.

Colours

Any strong whole colour including greys. White legs, above the hocks or knees, not desirable.

Note

The above breed standard and guideline is based on the Breed Standard and Guideline published in Irish Draught Horse Yearbook 1981 and on the Breed Standard as worded in O'Hare, N. (2002) *The Irish Sport Horse*. Readers wishing to consult the current official breed standard of the Irish Draught Horse Society should contact the Society. Contact details are given on the web page of the Society.

CONVERSION TABLE.

Hands to metric measurements (approximate)

Height in hands	Metres	Centimetres
12.2	1	27
12.3	1	30
13	1	32
13.1	1	34
13.2	1	37
13.3	1	40
14	1	42
14.1	1	44
14.2	1	47
14.3	1	50
15	1	52
15.1	1	55
15.2	1	57
15.3	1	60
16	1	62
16.1	1	65
16.2	1	68
16.3	1	70
17	1	72

Note:

1 hand = 4" (four inches). 12.2 = 12 hands and 2 inches, i. e. 50 inches (4' 2"). 12.3 = 12 hands and 3 inches. 12.35 = 12 hands and 3½ inches (ie, 51½"). Heights are measured from level ground to the top of a horse's withers. If the horse is shod, an allowance of 0.5" may be subtracted from the measured height to give the "official height".

INDEX

The index is divided into four sections: A for horses, B for people, C for places, D for general. Information shown on Figures 16-26 and in alphabetical lists on pages 105-6 is not completely indexed, neither are all places named on other Figures.

A. Names of horses

Abbeylara (476), 103, 109, 112.
Agherlow (810), 109.
Airmail (215), 95, 116.
All Moonshine (34), 68, 111, 113.
All the Diamonds (862), 104-5.
Amber Legend (864), 109.
Annaghdown Star (791), 105.
April Dandy (186), 73.
Arandora [Star] (247), 73.
Arctic Storm, 94-5, 103.
Ard Grandpa (807), 105.
Ardnacrushna (199),111.
Ardsallagh (260), 73.
Armada Star (566), 112.
Arthur, 93.
Atratus, 55.
Aughadown (565), 112.
Aughrim (380), 102.
Avondale (421), 111.

Ballingarry (152), 73, 102.
Ballingeary (477), 102.
Ballinrobe Boy (703), 118.
Ballybane Star (128), 73.
Ballybunnion (581), 102.
Ballyquirke (210), 73.
Ballyragget (153), 102.
Ballynoe Boy (596), 103, 120.
Baltimore (327), 102.
Banner County (197), 73.
Bantry Bay (63), 68, 95.
Bantry Bess (464), 95.
Bargyman (582), 102.

Barogue (2987), 93.
Bawnlahan (858), 112.
Ben Calverstown (832), 105.
Ben Purple (580), 98.
Biddens, 93.
Black Comet (52), 73, 95, 111-3, 121.
Black Diamond (226), 73.
Black Duke (35), 93, 98.
Black Garrett (36), 68 (shown on Fig.9 as Blue Garrett).
Black Prince (242), 106.
Blazing Star (53), 109.
Blue Garrett (36), see Black Garrett.
Blue Henry (744), 80.
Blue Peter (536), 80-1, 106, 113, 116.
Blue Rajah (759), 80.
Boston Burglar (6440), 107.
Branxholme, 53.
Brehon Law (59), 93, 103, 105-6, 112, 121.
Brian Boru (81), 73, 93.
Brian Og (94), 73, 93.
Bright Boy (303), 73, 111.
Bright Light (130), 73, 111-3.
Brightnet (216), 73, 112.
Bright Ray (144), 109.
Bright Star (58), 73, 111.
Brown Lad Lara (758), 109, 112.
Byerley Turk, 23, 41-2.

Cahirmee (258), 73.
Carrabawn View (751), 105.
Carrigboy (333), 102.
Carrigeen Lad (123), 72-4, 113.
Castana (837), 118.
Castlebawn (103), 93.
Castlehill Boy (243), 73.

Disclaimer
Although every reasonable effort has been made to ensure the accuracy of information presented in this book, the records that exist, especially pertaining to pedigrees, are such that errors may occur. Neither the author nor the publisher accept any legal responsibility for errors or omissions.